SCHOLASTIC
LITERACY SKILLS

Grammar and punctuation
Year 4

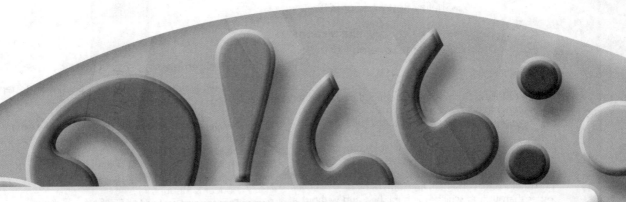

TERMS AND CONDITIONS

IMPORTANT – PERMITTED USE AND WARNINGS – READ CAREFULLY BEFORE USING

Minimum system requirements:

- PC or Mac with CD-ROM drive (16x speed recommended) and 512MB RAM
- P4 or G4 processor
- Windows 2000/XP/Vista or Mac OSX 10.3 or later

For all technical support queries, please phone Scholastic Customer Services on 0845 6039091.

Author

Huw Thomas

Editor

Rachel Mackinnon

Assistant editors

Vicky Butt and Margaret Eaton

CD-ROM design and development team

Joy Monkhouse, Anna Oliwa,
Micky Pledge, Rebecca Male, Allison Parry,
Shoo Fly Publishing and Haremi

Series designers

Shelley Best and Anna Oliwa

Book design team

Shelley Best and Sonja Bagley

Illustrations

Tim Archibold/Graham-Cameron Illustration

Designed using Adobe Indesign
Published by Scholastic Ltd, Villiers House,
Clarendon Avenue, Leamington Spa,
Warwickshire CV32 5PR
www.scholastic.co.uk

Printed by Bell & Bain Ltd, Glasgow
Text © 1999, 2008 Huw Thomas
© 2008 Scholastic Ltd
1 2 3 4 5 6 7 8 9 0   8 9 0 1 2 3 4 5 6 7

British Library Cataloguing-in-Publication Data
A catalogue record for this book is available from
the British Library.
ISBN 978-1407-10047-0

Acknowledgements

The publishers gratefully acknowledge permission to reproduce
the following copyright material:

Guardian News and Media Ltd for the use of an extract 'Match
Report' from *The Observer* – 28th June, 1998 © 1998, Guardian
News and Media Ltd.
Shirley Hughes for the use of text and illustrations from *It's too
frightening for me!* by Shirley Hughes © 1977, Shirley Hughes
(1977, Hodder & Stoughton).
Peters Fraser and Dunlop Ltd for the use of the poem 'Santa Fe'
by Michael Rosen from *Mind your own business* by Michael Rosen
© 1974, Michael Rosen (1974, Andre Deutsch).
Random House Group Ltd for the use of an extract from *Harvey
Angell* by Diana Hendry © 1997, Diana Hendry (1997, Red Fox).
Scholastic Australia Pty Ltd for the use of an extract from *Dead
Worried* by Moya Simons © 1996, Moya Simons (1996, Omnibus
Books).

Every effort has been made to trace copyright holders for the
works reproduced in this book, and the publishers apologise for
any inadvertent omissions.

Extracts from Primary National Strategy's Primary Framework for
Literacy (2006) www.standards.dfes.gov.uk/primaryframework ©
Crown copyright. Reproduced under the terms of the Click Use
Licence.

Contents

Chapter 1
Verbs

Chapter 2
Adjectives

Chapter 3
Apostrophes and hyphens

Chapter 4
Organising sentences

Chapter 5
Changing words

Chapter 6
Adverbs

Introduction

The Scholastic Literacy Skills: Grammar and punctuation series

This series works from the premise that grammar and punctuation can be interesting and dynamic – but on one condition. The condition is that the teaching of these aspects of grammar must be related to real texts and practical activities that experiment with language, investigate the use of language in real contexts and find the ways in which grammar and punctuation are used in our day-to-day talk, writing and reading. This book encourages children to look back at their written work and find ways to revise and improve it.

Teaching grammar and punctuation

'As a writer I know that I must select studiously the nouns, pronouns, verbs, adverbs, etcetera, and by a careful syntactical arrangement make readers laugh, reflect or riot.'
Maya Angelou

The *Scholastic Literacy Skills: Grammar and punctuation* series equips teachers with resources and subject training enabling them to teach grammar and punctuation. The focus of the resource is on what is sometimes called sentence-level work, so called because grammar and punctuation primarily involve the construction and understanding of sentences.

Many teachers bring with them a lot of past memories when they approach the teaching of grammar. Some will remember school grammar lessons as the driest of subjects, involving drills and parsing, and will wonder how they can make it exciting for their own class. At the other end of the spectrum, some will have received relatively little formal teaching of grammar at school. In other words, there are teachers who, when asked to teach clause structure or prepositions, feel at a bit of a loss. They are being asked to teach things they are not confident with themselves. Even worse, they think they should be confident in these things.

Grammar can evoke lethargy, fear, irritation, pedantry and despondency. Yet as can be seen from the above comment by Maya Angelou, we have one of the greatest modern writers presenting her crafting of sentences as an exciting and tactical process that has a powerful effect on her readers. Can this be the grammar that makes teachers squirm or run?

About the product

The book is divided into six chapters. Each chapter looks at a different aspect of grammar and punctuation and is divided into five sections. Each section includes teachers' notes – objective, background knowledge, notes on how to use the photocopiable pages, further ideas and what's on the CD-ROM – and two to three photocopiable pages.

Posters

Each chapter has two posters. These posters are related to the contents of the chapter and should be displayed and used for reference throughout the work on the chapter. The poster notes (on the chapter opening page) offer suggestions for how they could be used. There are black and white versions in the book and full-colour versions on the CD-ROM for you to print out or display on your whiteboard.

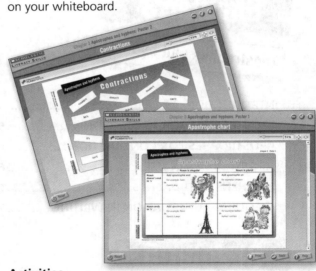

Activities

Each section contains two to three activities. These activities all take the form of a photocopiable page which is in the book. Each photocopiable page is also included on the CD-ROM for you to display or print out (these pages also provide answers where appropriate). Over thirty of the photocopiable pages have linked interactive activities on the CD-ROM. These interactive activities are designed to act as starter activities to the lesson, giving whole-class support on the information being taught. However, they can also work equally well as plenary activities, reviewing the work the children have just completed.

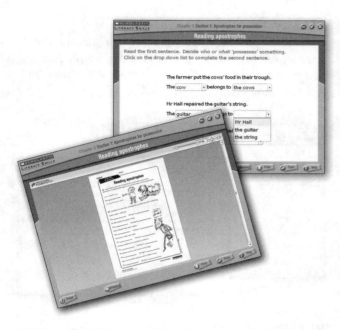

Writing sections

The final section in each chapter focuses on writing. It differs slightly in layout to the other sections – rather than teaching children new skills, you are encouraging them to practise the ones they have already learned throughout the chapter and to use them in writing. There are two photocopiable pages in each of these sections; many of them are writing frames or provide prompts to encourage the children to write. As with the other sections, a number of further ideas are also included, which provide imaginative and interesting starting points for writing.

Using the CD-ROM

Below are brief guidance notes for using the CD-ROM. For more detailed information, see **How to use** on the start-up screen, or **Help** on the relevant screen for information about that page.

The CD-ROM follows the structure of the book and contains:

- All of the photocopiable pages.
- All of the poster pages in full colour.
- Photocopiable pages (with answers where appropriate).
- Over thirty interactive on-screen activities linked to the photocopiable pages.

Getting started

To begin using the CD-ROM, simply place it in your CD- or DVD-ROM drive. Although the CD-ROM should auto-run, if it fails to do so, navigate to the drive and double-click on the red **Start** icon.

Start-up screen

The start-up screen is the first screen that appears. Here you can access: terms and conditions, registration links, how to use the CD-ROM and credits. If you agree to the terms and conditions, click **Start** to continue.

Main menu

The main menu provides links to all of the chapters or all of the resources. Clicking on the relevant **Chapter** icon will take you to the chapter screen where you can access the posters and the chapter's sections. Clicking on **All resources** will take you to a list of all the resources, where you can search by key word or chapter for a specific resource.

Section screen

Upon choosing a section from the chapter screen, you are taken to a list of resources for that section. Here you can access all of the photocopiable pages related to that section as well as the linked interactive activities.

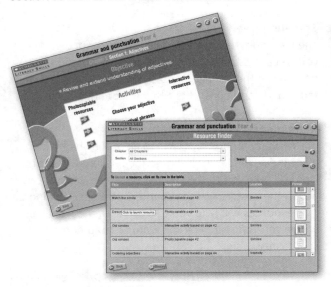

Resource finder

The **Resource finder** lists all of the resources on the CD-ROM. You can:

- Select a chapter and/or section by selecting the appropriate title from the drop-down menus.
- Search for key words by typing them into the search box.
- Scroll up or down the list of resources to locate the required resource.
- To launch a resource, simply click on its row on the screen.

Navigation

The resources (poster pages, photocopiable pages and interactive activities) all open in separate windows on top of the menu screen. This means that you can have more than one resource open at the same time. To close a resource, click on the **x** in the top right-hand corner of the screen. To return to the menu screen you can either close or minimise a resource.

Closing a resource will not close the program. However, if you are in a menu screen, then clicking on the **x** will close the program. To return to a previous menu screen, you need to click on the **Back** button.

Glossary

Most of the interactive activities link to a glossary. The glossary will open in a separate window. Simply click first on the desired headletter and then on the word to reveal its definition.

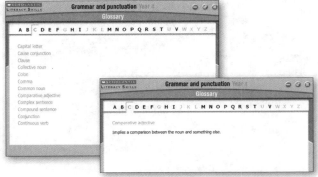

Whiteboard tools

The CD-ROM comes with its own set of whiteboard tools for use on any whiteboard. These include:

- Pen tool
- Highlighter tool
- Eraser
- Sticky note

Click on the **Tools** button at the foot of the screen to access these tools.

Printing

Print the resources by clicking on the **Print** button. The photocopiable pages print as full A4 portrait pages, but please note if you have a landscape photocopiable page or poster you need to set the orientation to landscape in your print preferences. The interactive activities will print what is on the screen. For a full A4 printout you need to set the orientation to landscape in your print preferences.

Framework objectives

Page	Section	Literacy skills objective	Strand 6: Know and apply common spelling rules.	Strand 7: Use knowledge of different organisational features of texts to find information effectively.	Strand 7: Explain how writers use figurative and expressive language to create images and atmosphere.	Strand 9: Show imagination through the language used to create emphasis, humour, atmosphere or suspense.	Strand 9: Choose and combine words, images and other features for particular effects.	Strand 10: Use adverbs and conjunctions to establish cohesion within paragraphs.	Strand 11: Use commas to mark clauses, and use the apostrophe for possession.	Strand 11: Clarify meaning and point of view by using varied sentence structure.	Chapter
12	Verbs	Revise and investigate verb tenses.	✓			✓					Chapter 1
16	Tense and purpose	Develop awareness of how tense relates to purpose and structure of text.		✓		✓					Chapter 1
20	Verb power	Identify and use powerful verbs.				✓					Chapter 1
24	Verbs in literature	Identify and use powerful verbs.				✓	✓				Chapter 1
28	Writing verbs	Develop use of verbs in writing.				✓	✓				Chapter 1
35	Adjectives	Revise and extend understanding of adjectives.					✓				Chapter 2
39	Similes	Understand the use of adjectives in figurative language.				✓	✓				Chapter 2
43	Intensity	Learn the degrees of intensity that adjectives can denote.				✓	✓				Chapter 2
47	Comparative and superlative	Understand and use comparative and superlative adjectives.	✓				✓				Chapter 2
51	Developing adjectives	Develop the use of adjectives in writing.				✓	✓				Chapter 2
58	Apostrophes for possession	Identify possessive apostrophes in reading and writing and to whom or what they refer.	✓						✓		Chapter 3
62	Apostrophes for contraction	Distinguish between apostrophes for possession and contraction.	✓						✓		Chapter 3
66	Apostrophes in use	Understand the uses of the apostrophe in reading and writing.							✓		Chapter 3
70	Hyphens and dashes	Identify and begin to understand the use of hyphens and dashes.				✓				✓	Chapter 3
74	Refining punctuation in writing	Consolidate the use of punctuation marks in writing.								✓	Chapter 3

Framework objectives

Page	Section	Literacy skills objective	Strand 6: Know and apply common spelling rules.	Strand 7: Use knowledge of different organisational features of texts to find information effectively.	Strand 7: Explain how writers use figurative and expressive language to create images and	Strand 9: Show imagination through the language used to create emphasis, humour, atmosphere	Strand 9: Choose and combine words, images and other features for particular effects.	Strand 10: Use adverbs and conjunctions to establish cohesion within paragraphs.	Strand 11: Use commas to mark clauses, and use the apostrophe for possession.	Strand 11: Clarify meaning and point of view by using varied sentence structure.
81	Revisiting punctuation	Identify common punctuation marks.							✓	✓
85	Commas and sentences	Practise the use of commas separating grammatical boundaries within sentences.							✓	✓
89	Colon and semicolon	Recognise colons and semicolons and respond to them when reading.						✓	✓	✓
93	Connectives	Understand the way in which clauses are connected.						✓	✓	✓
97	Organising sentence writing	Apply the various sentence features used to organise sentences to writing.								✓
104	Verb endings	Learn the ways in which verbs and verb endings can change.	✓							
108	Comparative endings	Understand the ways in which comparative endings change.	✓				✓			
112	Pluralisation	Understand the ways in which noun endings change for plurals.	✓							
116	Changes and word class	Use changes that can be made in words to identify word class.	✓							
120	Choose the 'write' words	Apply, and develop the use of, rules for the changing of words in writing.	✓			✓	✓			
127	Identifying adverbs	Learn to identify adverbs, noticing where they occur in sentences and how they are used to modify the verbs.	✓					✓		
131	The 'ly' suffix	Identify common adverbs with 'ly' suffix.	✓					✓		
135	Classifying adverbs	Collect and classify examples of adverbs.					✓	✓		
139	Changing adverbs	Investigate the effects of substituting adverbs in particular contexts.					✓	✓		
143	Incredibly useful verbs	Develop the use of adverbs in writing.				✓	✓			

Chapter 4 · Chapter 5 · Chapter 6

Chapter 1

Verbs

Introduction

This chapter looks at the tenses of verbs and at the range of verbs that can be used. It also looks at the way verbs are matched to the context in which they are used, such as the link between a particular type of text and the verb tenses that will be used in it, and the uses of verbs in literature. The concluding writing activities then gather this awareness of verbs and promotes the use of a wide range of examples from this word class in writing.

Poster notes

Alternative verbs (page 10)
As children look at the selection and effect of various verbs, this poster provides a basic thesaurus with which they can select the appropriate term for an action. It can be used as a tool for writing or as a way of spicing up sentences when redrafting.

Past and present tenses (page 11)
This poster provides some examples of tense changes. It can be used as a teaching poster – if the columns are covered over in turn, children can be asked to supply past tenses for present tenses and vice versa.

In this chapter

Verbs page 12	Revise and investigate verb tenses.
Tense and purpose page 16	Develop awareness of how tense relates to purpose and structure of text.
Verb power page 20	Identify and use powerful verbs.
Verbs in literature page 24	Identify and use powerful verbs.
Writing verbs page 28	Develop use of verbs in writing.

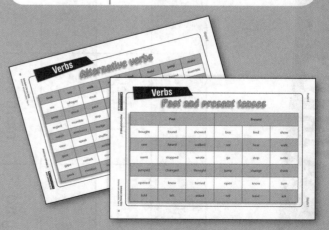

Verbs

Alternative verbs

look	say	walk	run	find	hold	jump	make
see	whisper	stroll	dart	discover	grip	bound	assemble
peep	shout	pace	dash	unearth	grasp	spring	create
regard	mumble	step	scarper	disclose	seize	hop	construct
watch	announce	trudge	sprint	acquire	grab	leap	produce
view	speak	shuffle	scramble	recover	clutch	pounce	manufacture
gaze	tell	amble	scurry	spot	possess	bounce	build
gape	remark	move	hurry	learn	clasp	vault	generate
gawk	mention	march	race	notice	squeeze	lurch	fashion

Verbs
Past and present tenses

Present						
show	find		buy			
walk	hear		see			
write	stop		go			
think	change		jump			
turn	know		open			
ask	leave		tell			

Past						
showed		found		bought		
walked		heard		saw		
wrote		stopped		went		
thought		changed		jumped		
turned		knew		opened		
asked		left		told		

Verbs

Objective

Revise and investigate verb tenses.

Background knowledge

Tense shows the timing of a verb. It is the way a verb changes to show whether an action happened in the present (*I run*) or the past (*I ran*). The word alters to denote when something happens.

In the English language there are two simple tenses:

● **Present tense:** the action is occurring now (*I walk*)

● **Past tense:** the action occurred previously. The common ending for past-tense verbs is 'ed' (*I walked*).

For these two tenses the verb itself can alter. There is a third, more complex tense, this is:

● **Future tense:** it is made in a compound form. This means another word is added to set a verb in the future, so in the above examples the simple present has the word 'will' added. This creates the compound forms *will run* and *will walk*.

Activities

The activities focus on spoken sentences. They look at the type of things children say and ask them to reflect on the tenses they are using. This topic should involve a lot of discussion, with groups analysing examples from their own language use.

● **Photocopiable page 13 'Past, present or future'**
This activity revises the three simple tense forms. Ask the children to cut out the sentences, then encourage them to say the sentences out loud before sorting them into past, present and future tenses. They may want to make up some cards of their own, recording additional sentences that can be spoken aloud, then placing them in the correct group.

● **Photocopiable page 14 'Change the tense'**
Ask the children to choose eight sentences from the ones they have worked with on photocopiable page 13 (one has already been done for them). Explain that each sentence should be written in the correct box, then written out again for the other two tenses. Some children may need to be directed towards particular sentences that gave them a challenge or stimulated their thinking in the earlier task.

● **Photocopiable page 15 'Using tenses'**
By using verbs in their tenses in this activity, the children can develop their understanding of how the tenses feature in certain types of sentence and the way the form of the verb indicates its tense. As an extra challenge, the children could try including more than one of the verbs shown in a sentence.

Further ideas

● **Role-play:** In a group of four, two of the children in the group can listen to the other two acting out a conversation. It could be about things they enjoy or places they have visited. As they speak, the listeners make notes of the different tenses used. This will usually lead to the two role-players steering the conversation around the tenses and even pausing while notes are made, but it will still provide an insight into the use of tenses at different points in a conversation.

● **Spelling:** As the children engage in these activities, they may begin to comment on the spelling patterns evident in the various tenses. These can be highlighted and irregular verbs can also be noted.

What's on the CD-ROM

On the CD-ROM you will find:
● Printable versions of all three photocopiable pages.
● Answers to 'Past, present or future'.
● Interactive version of 'Past, present or future'.

Verbs

Past, present or future

■ Cut out the sentences. Say them aloud, then sort them into three piles.

Sentences that happened in the past.

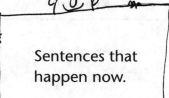

Sentences that happen now.

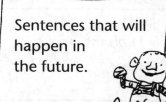

Sentences that will happen in the future.

I will ask the teacher.	She will write a letter.	I saw my friend.
I think about stories.	You know the answer.	I brought my lunch box.
He writes a note.	I will ride my bike.	I leave the pips.
I heard music.	I found a pencil.	I will see you tomorrow.
You stopped moving.	I change my socks.	They will have their tea.

Illustrations © 1999, Tim Archibold.

Name:

Verbs

Change the tense

■ Choose some sentences from photocopiable page 13 'Past, present or future'. Write each sentence in the correct column. Rewrite it in the other two tenses.

	Past	Present	Future
1	I thought about stories.	I think about stories.	I will think about stories.
2			
3			
4			
5			
6			
7			
8			

PHOTOCOPIABLE

Verbs

Using tenses

■ Look at these verbs.

run	ran	make
made	found	
find	says	said

■ Try to write **eight** sentences, each one containing a different verb chosen from the box above.

1 _____

2 _____

3 _____

4 _____

5 _____

6 _____

7 _____

8 _____

■SCHOLASTIC
www.scholastic.co.uk   **PHOTOCOPIABLE**   **Scholastic Literacy Skills**
Grammar and punctuation: Year 4   **15**

Tense and purpose

Develop awareness of how tense relates to purpose and structure of text.

Background knowledge

Different tenses are commonly used in different types of writing. A weather report will set sentences in the predicted future. A diary will usually record events that have happened in the past.

The recount of events in a narrative will tend to be written in the past tense (for example, *I walked out onto the moor in the darkness…*). Explanatory reports are often in the present tense (for example, a house survey might state, *The ground floor is in a good state of repair…*). Forecasts and predictions will be written in the future tense (for example, *It will be showery at first…*).

These are general rules. There are exceptions (such as narratives written in the present tense) but an understanding of the varied tenses used in different types of writing provides an insight into various text types. After all, it is obvious that a forecast, whether it is about the weather or the outcome of a football game, will be written in the future tense.

Activities

As children undertake these activities, it needs to be stressed that the text extracts are not just examples of the tenses at work. Throughout their work, draw the children's attention to the types of texts they are analysing. For instance, as they look at tenses in a magazine, they should be encouraged to look at different examples at home – they may find a present-tense report about a film star, for example. As they find their own examples of the text types, encourage the children to apply the activities to them.

● **Photocopiable page 17 'Write start'**
Ask the children to think ahead to the type of writing they will be doing in each of the three sections of the sheet – whether it will need to be written in the past tense, the present tense or the future tense. It is important that the three examples are written in close proximity to each other, to reinforce the differences in the tenses. Follow the activity with a plenary discussion, focusing on the thoughts the children had about the opening lines they were writing – the verbs they used and the reasons they used particular tenses.

● **Photocopiable page 18 'Magazine extracts'**
These example extracts show the way different texts use certain tenses. To give the activity a more contemporary slant, they can be supplemented by extracts from a current pop magazine. The children can analyse the tenses used in the texts and reflect on how they suit the purpose of the writing.

● **Photocopiable page 19 'Tense test'**
One way to encourage children to change the tense in the sentences is to start by saying them aloud and adding the word 'Yesterday', 'Today' or 'Tomorrow' to the beginning (for example, *Yesterday the children laughed when the clown fell over*). They can then say the sentence using the alternative starter word (*Tomorrow the children will…*) and rework the sentence accordingly, finding the words they alter – the verbs.

Further ideas

● **Reword the text:** A number of the texts explored in this activity could be reworded. Ask the children to change the tenses of sentences – for example, they could rework a forecast into the past tense. This will often demonstrate just how much the tense supports the purpose of the original text.

● **Television excerpts:** Record three five-minute excerpts from the television (copyright permitting). Examples could include a block of adverts, a short scene from a soap opera, a part of a children's information programme. When the children watch the excerpts, ask them to listen carefully to try to find examples of the different tenses used in each of them.

What's on the CD-ROM

On the CD-ROM you will find:
● Printable versions of all three photocopiable pages.
● Answers to 'Magazine extracts' and 'Tense test'.
● Interactive version of 'Magazine extracts'.

Tense and purpose

Write start

■ Write some opening lines for different texts in the boxes below.
■ Look at the verbs you have used in each piece of writing. Fill in the grid.

a diary extract about things that happened yesterday at school	a recipe for making toast or a cup of tea

a plan for what you will do in your next school holiday		
	Type of writing	**Tense used**
	diary	
	recipe	
	holiday plan	

Name:

Tense and purpose

Magazine extracts

■ Here are some extracts from a pop magazine. Pick out verbs and verb phrases with a highlighter pen. Note down the main tense used in each extract.

Queen Sweep

Pop group Sweeper flew in to London this week to receive their 'London Hits' award for best group. They also won the award for 'Best song' and came second in the 'Best video' award. But the band were more interested in other things. 'We wanted to see the Queen,' lead singer Sam told reporters. 'Yeh! We thought it would be cool and that she would pop into the party. She probably went to the wrong place.'

main tense: _____

Widdering Heights

The news is out. Singer Phil Widders, pop's wild child, is scared of something. Phil tells us he hates tall buildings. 'I hate heights,' he says, 'but it is a strange sort of fear. I can happily stand on a tall building. I hate it when I stand outside one and look up at the top. It terrifies me.'
Hmmmmm.

main tense: _____

Buzz's new single, 'Melting'

Pop group Buzz have another hit with this one. Many say it is their best song ever. It features in the hit film 'Slides' and includes guitarist Matt doing a violin solo!

main tense: _____

New single from Mice Girls

Record shops will need space outside the doors on 14 July. The new Mice Girls single will be released on that date. The girls will fly into London for the release and will appear on the roof of 'Majestic Records' in the city, where they will perform the single for fans.

main tense: _____

Tense and purpose

Tense test

The **tense test** can show whether a particular word is a verb.
Look at this sentence:

   I saw a saw.

Say the sentence in a different tense.

   I see a saw.

The word that changes tense is a verb.

   I (see) a saw.

sometimes words look like verbs but are actually nouns

■ Look at these sentences and find which words are used as a verb. The first one has been done for you.

When I play football I run very fast.

Verbs	Changed tense
play	played
run	ran

The toffee is sticky so we chew it a lot.

Verbs	Changed tense

The children laughed when the clown fell over.

Verbs	Changed tense

On Saturday we will shop for shoes and buy ones we like.

Verbs	Changed tense

We went on a hunt and found some lost treasure.

Verbs	Changed tense

Our teacher sits and listens to our moans about school.

Verbs	Changed tense

I go to the shop and buy a chew.

Verbs	Changed tense

I made a promise and I kept it.

Verbs	Changed tense

Illustrations © 1999, Tim Archibold.

■ SCHOLASTIC
www.scholastic.co.uk   **PHOTOCOPIABLE**   **Scholastic Literacy Skills**
Grammar and punctuation: Year 4   **19**

Verb power

Identify and use powerful verbs.

Background knowledge

Verb choice can be an important feature in the composition of a piece of writing. If an entrance into a room is recorded as *sauntering into the room,* this conjures up a very different picture from *storming into the room.*

If you take a particular sentence, there may be a verb that does not fit in with the tone of what is being expressed, for example, *I stormed gently into the room.* While this type of incongruous verb can sound odd, it can also be used to the children's advantage as a way of making a sentence more striking and interesting.

Activities

Exploring this area of language with children involves looking at the possible verbs that can fit into a sentence and analysing selected examples. The activities encourage children to reflect on particular verb choices and to look for alternative words that can work in a particular way.

● **Photocopiable page 21 'Choose a different verb'**
Looking at the atmosphere and setting of the passage, the children can use words from the verb box to develop it. They may suggest some interesting combinations of words (for example, *The tree ruffled in the wind*). There are more verbs suggested than there are words to be changed in the story, so the children should not be under any pressure to find correct solutions in this task. They are being encouraged to experiment with possibilities. Indeed, a diversity of results makes the activity more worthwhile.

● **Photocopiable page 22 'Change the verb'**
The children will need to say the sentences aloud, sometimes saying them a few times as they rework them to natural language. Different children may make different changes to the sentences to make them sound right. The

most natural change to *When I went on the train I leave my umbrella* would be *When I went on the train I left my umbrella.* However, a child might change it to the grammatically consistent *When I go on the train I leave my umbrella.* This raises questions as to why anyone would deliberately lose an umbrella, but any variations like this can be compared and discussed as alternative ways of reworking the tense.

● **Photocopiable page 23 'Possibilities'**
As adults write, they often stop to consider the best word to use in a particular situation. They weigh up the tactfulness and power of particular words. In this set of verb choices, the children are asked to consider some of the verbs that could complete a sentence, collecting three possibilities for the same space in a sentence. Once they have finished the activity, they could compare their selected verbs with those that their friends chose and record next to each sentence any interesting possibilities they missed.

Further ideas

● **Thesauruses:** Ask the children to use thesauruses to collate lists of alternative ways of denoting particular actions or happenings. They can also refer to the examples on the 'Alternative verbs' poster (see page 10).
● **Verb-power list:** The children can make lists of particularly powerful verbs they encounter in their reading. These lists could be used to compile an edited whole-class list of the best verbs that have been found.
● **Right verb in the right place:** Find out, as a class, how different types of verbs are used in different contexts. For example, how do verbs that are used when the children are talking in the playground differ from verbs that are used in a letter to parents from the headteacher?

 **What's on the CD-ROM**

On the CD-ROM you will find:
● Printable versions of all three photocopiable pages.
● Answers to 'Change the verb'.
● Interactive versions of 'Choose a different verb' and 'Possibilities'.

Verb power

Choose a different verb

■ Read this piece of writing. Find the verbs in it and try to improve them. Choose words from the lists and write the new words above the ones in the passage (cross out the words you are replacing).

crept	clattered	banged	fled	fumbled	stepped
squealed	swept	swayed	pushed	searched	wheeled
whispered	moaned	stuffed	smashed	spied	padded
swung	ruffled	bounded	leaped	whistled	hurried

The postwoman walked up to the creepy house. The tree moved in the wind. The

shutters closed together in the icy gust. The wind went through the chimney pots.

A cat went up the path. It jumped through the window. The postwoman looked

for the right letter. Inside the house the cat pushed a vase off the

table. The vase broke on the floor. The postwoman

put the letter through the letter box.

She turned around to go. The cat saw

the crack of light from the door. The

door moved open. "Eeeeeek!" the

hinges went.

The postwoman ran.

Verb power

Change the verb

■ Change the verb in each of these sentences so that it makes sense. Think about the tense of the verb. The first one has been done for you.

I found the shoe I lose.

I found the shoe I lost.

Last week I see my aunty when she cycles to our house.

Tomorrow we will go to the shop and bought some new shoes.

When I went on the train I leave my umbrella.

Every time we do PE I jumped off the wall bars.

We started a game of football, then we stop when the bell ring.

We will turn off the TV because there was nothing on.

I write a letter and then I posted it.

My brother wakes up late and rushed to school.

I knew a game so I teach it to my friends.

Verb power

Possibilities

■ For each of the sentences below, list **two** possible verbs. Try to think of some powerful ones or some unusual ones. The first one has been done for you.

The dog | ran / fled | from the burning house.

I | _____ | round my room to find shoes.

Our baby | _____ | because he was hungry.

The spaceship | _____ | into space.

The thief | _____ | when he saw the police car.

A firework | _____ | in the sky.

The mountain climber | _____ | onto the ledge.

My gran | _____ | when she is in a bad mood.

The monster | _____ | out of the cave.

I dropped a glass and it | _____ | .

Verbs in literature

Identify and use powerful verbs.

Background knowledge

Stylistics is the study of language in literature. It looks at how features of the language of a text relate to the meaning a reader draws from it. One interesting vein for exploration in this subject is the use of unusual combinations of words to create images. A metaphor involves one thing being described in terms of another, something with which it is not normally associated. Hence when a character in Shakespeare's *Romeo and Juliet* says, 'Come, we burn daylight, ho!' he conjures up an image, using the verb 'burn' to describe the using up of daylight.

Activities

Literature can provide a rich resource for developing children's awareness of powerful verb uses. The pieces of literature selected for these activities contain interesting and effective uses of verbs.

Photocopiable page 25 'Fill the gaps'

This activity uses a cloze exercise; the extract is taken from *Harvey Angell* by Diana Hendry (Red Fox) – see CD-ROM for the solution. It can be done in two stages. Initially the children can be asked to have a go at thinking of possible verbs that could be used in the text, filling in the spaces in pencil. If you then reveal the verbs used by the author, writing them on a flipchart in random order, the children can try to see where they could fit. By comparing their choices with the original, they can see how verbs can be used in interesting and powerful ways.

● **Photocopiable page 26 'Different ways of saying'**

The powerful use of verbs in figurative and imaginative language is explored through this activity. The children can complete these sentences in any number of ways; they are deliberately given more words than there are spaces, so that they will be able to generate interesting and imaginative combinations.

● **Photocopiable page 27 'Night clouds'**

Through this activity the children explore the creative edge of language, looking at the use of verbs to denote the actions of the moonlit clouds across the night sky. It takes them beyond a straightforward identification of the verbs in the poem to a consideration of the effect of the verbs used.

Further ideas

● **Text verbs:** Ask the children to look through a story or a poem and list some of the verbs they think are particular to that text. For example, in Maurice Sendak's *Where the Wild Things Are* (Bodley Head) Max *makes* mischief, he *sails* away on a boat, he *stares* into the eyes of the wild things. The verbs take on a particular association with the story.

● **Unusual combinations:** Ask the children to look at a particular action, such as a cat rubbing against its owner's leg. They can consider the usual verbs for the action and then try out some unusual combinations (such as *The cat swam against its owner's leg*).

● **Collecting combinations:** Particularly effective uses of powerful verbs can be recorded on a chart or in a small book. Ask the children to keep a look out for them in their reading and to jot down interesting examples.

 **What's on the CD-ROM**

On the CD-ROM you will find:
● Printable versions of all three photocopiable pages.
● Answers to 'Fill the gaps'.
● Interactive versions of 'Fill the gaps' and 'Different ways of saying'.

Verbs in literature

Fill the gaps

Harvey Angell is the story of a strange character, Harvey, who comes to live at the sad house of Henry and his Aunt Agatha. Henry is fascinated by Harvey and wants to know where he goes, very early each morning. In this extract he decides to follow him.

■   Read the passage and guess what the missing verbs could be. Write them in the spaces.

Henry _____ his alarm clock very quickly before it could _____

Aunt Agatha. He _____ still, listening. A sleepy silence _____ the

house only _____ by the occasional snorting snore from Aunt Agatha's

room. Then there was movement! Creaks on the stairs! The sound of someone

_____ in the kitchen. Harvey Angell was up and about…

Henry _____ out of bed, _____ on his jeans and shirt and

_____ . He would _____ until he _____ the front door

close, then he would _____ twenty, then he would _____ off,

_____ Harvey Angell. Henry's mouth _____ very dry.

He _____ he could _____ into the kitchen

for a drink of water.

Diana Hendry

Text © 1997, Diana Hendry; illustrations © 1999, Tim Archibold.

Name:

Verbs in literature

Different ways of saying

Metaphors involve using words to describe things they do not usually describe. If we say 'Leo is confused', we could take the word 'drowning', which is usually associated with being in water,

and make an interesting image 'Leo was drowning in confusion'.

■ Cut out the verbs. See how many are suitable for each of the spaces. Write down some of the interesting sentences you make using different verbs.

swam	barked	dodged	smiled	flew	galloped	sidled
splattered	scuttled	screamed	slithered	slouched	stretched	hurtled

The cat		in the streetlight.
The runner		round the track.
My sister		into school.
The old man		with laughter.
Raindrops		down the window pane.
A mouse		round the pipes.
The sun		on the field.
A football		through the window.

Illustrations © 1999, Tim Archibold.

Verbs in literature

Night clouds

The white mares of the moon rush along the sky

Beating their golden hoofs upon the glass Heavens;

The white mares of the moon are all standing on their hind legs

Pawing at the green porcelain doors of the remote Heavens.

Fly, mares!

Strain your utmost,

Scatter the milky dust of stars,

Or the tiger sun will leap upon you and destroy you

With one lick of his vermilion tongue.

Amy Lowell (1874–1925)

■ Look at the verbs in the poem. What sort of action or happening do they make you think of? Write some notes about them on a separate sheet of paper.

Illustrations © 1999, Tim Archibold.

Writing verbs

Develop use of verbs in writing.

Writing focus

Having secured their understanding of the function and tense of verbs, these activities focus on the children gathering a range of powerful verbs for writing.

Skills to writing

● Imagining verbs

Building up the stock of verbs that children can draw on for their writing is one of the key ways of enriching the language they use. However, you cannot simply impose a list of new verbs on children. This just ends up with the words being used inappropriately or sounding stilted and wooden. To expand children's verb bank it is important to allow them to become familiar with the new words, say them aloud and enjoy the sound. Verbs such as *pounded* are a pleasure to say. You also need to make sure children know their meaning: *pounded* isn't a straight synonym of *knocked*, it's a particular type of knock. A good way for children to learn the meaning of verbs is to picture or act them (have a go at *pounding*). To help children consolidate the information, try out the words in shared, modelled and guided writing – the verbs need to be given an airing!

● Verb collection

Maintain a class collection of powerful verbs. Keeping a ring binder can be a useful way of recording verbs collected from a range of sources. As a rule of thumb, every reading from a story or poem should net at least one addition for the collection.

● Verb hunts

This activity is linked to the one above. As a filler activity at the end of reading time, ask the children to hunt for new and interesting verbs in their reading. It is not uncommon for them to find ones where they aren't certain of the meaning but have used context to gain a rough idea. This sort of hunting activity can be turned into a challenge – such as covering a 100-square wallchart with sticky notes and building up a collection of 'This month's 100 best verbs'.

● Tense and text type

Encourage the children to look at the tenses in texts. As they encounter different texts, ask them to keep a tally of how the texts use different tenses. Ask why such language suits the purpose – for example, there's a good reason why a newsletter often recounts in the past tense and a trip letter anticipates an outing in the future. One interesting feature to look out for is the way a single text can mix the tenses: for example, a letter that says what the class have been doing could then slip into a future class assembly.

● Verbs and planning

Focus on verbs as tools in the planning of texts. In narrative writing they provide an effective way of sketching out a storyline (losing – seeking – finding being one of the simplest examples, yet a vital story planner).*Story Structure Architect* (Victoria Lynn Schmidt, Writers Digest Books), written for story writing, provides an interesting example of some of the basic story structures around which children can build their narrative.

● Explanations

Verbs are vital to the reading, planning and writing of explanation texts. The cause and effect process, where one verb leads to another, provides a way of unpicking a process and preparing to write about it.

Activities

● Photocopiable page 30 'Verb changes'

The children can use this photocopiable sheet to record the changes made to the passage in 'Choose a different verb' (page 21). Alternatively, they can use the grid as a way of reviewing another piece of writing in which they have altered the verbs, using it as a means of reflecting on their own story writing.

● Photocopiable page 31 'Twelve verbs to use'

This photocopiable sheet can be used as a stimulus in planning, a means of challenging children to widen their verb use, or a starter to children's own verb hunting. It can either be used as a poster, or the children can keep it as a checklist for their use of the verbs. Alternatively, cut out the rectangles and challenge the children to pick two out of a hat – then get to know and use them. It provides some examples of powerful verbs that the children could use in their writing, following the notes above about first becoming familiar with them.

Write on

- **Create verb-o-saurus posters**

Ask the children to devise posters for common verbs they will use in their writing, gathering new examples and writing examples of their use. If they have gathered these from a text, ask them to quote the source.

- **Manifesto**

The children can write up the changes they would make were they given the mandate to do so. What would they do if they were placed in charge of the school? What if they were placed in charge of education policy? What if they took over the country? Ask them to build up their future tense promises of 'What we will do'.

- **Word processing**

The children can use the thesaurus facility to develop texts they have typed on the computer. This is a classic example of a context where the new words are often just generated, so children need to look up the new suggestions in a dictionary. However, the resultant habit of using the relevant keystroke can guide the children to some effective word choices.

- **Unusual verbs**

Together, gather verbs that are commonly associated with one topic that can be applied to another. A useful consideration is to think of the image conjured up when certain unusual verbs are applied to a person. *Slithered* is a verb that conjures up a reptilian image, so what image does this conjure up when it is applied to a teacher *slithering* into the classroom? What about a child *bouncing* down the corridor or someone *dripping* down the corridor? This sort of innovative experiment can make for some interesting word usage.

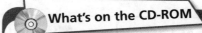

What's on the CD-ROM

On the CD-ROM you will find:
- Printable versions of both photocopiable pages.
- Interactive version of 'Twelve verbs to use'.

Name:

Writing verbs

Verb changes

■ Look at a piece of text in which you have changed the verbs. In this table record the original verb and the new verb you have chosen.

Original verb	My verb	Why mine is better

Writing verbs

Twelve verbs to use

■ Can you use these interesting verbs in your writing?

yelled	crept	flounced
explored	gasped	fled
leapt	uncovered	scrunched
seized	scrambled	startled

Chapter 2

Adjectives

Introduction

Adjectives can really fire up children's minds because they are so delightfully unnecessary. Obviously we need a few to function in life, but many are above and beyond basic language; children can enjoy the idea that there are great ways of describing everything they speak and write about. This chapter secures the notion that adjectives do a particular job, but then a crucial aim in the activities that involve choosing and using adjectives is that children's experience should widen, including the joy of similes.

In this chapter

Poster notes

Fruity adjectives (page 33)

This collection of adjectives is aimed at words beyond the immediate examples that spring to mind. The idea is that children should familiarise themselves with these and, at some point, try using a few. Highlight one and invite the children to try to use it in speech over the course of a day. The main aim is to have fun trying out some words that sound so fruity!

Jabberwocky (page 34)

As they look at the poem, children can pick out the words they think are functioning as adjectives. Examples include 'brillig' and 'mimsy'. Once they have listed the 'adjectives', they can try imagining what sort of qualities each one might be describing.

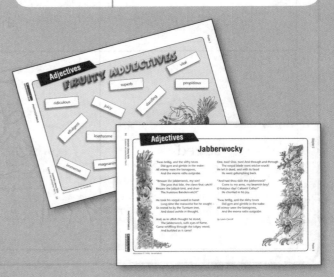

Adjectives

FRUITY ADJECTIVES

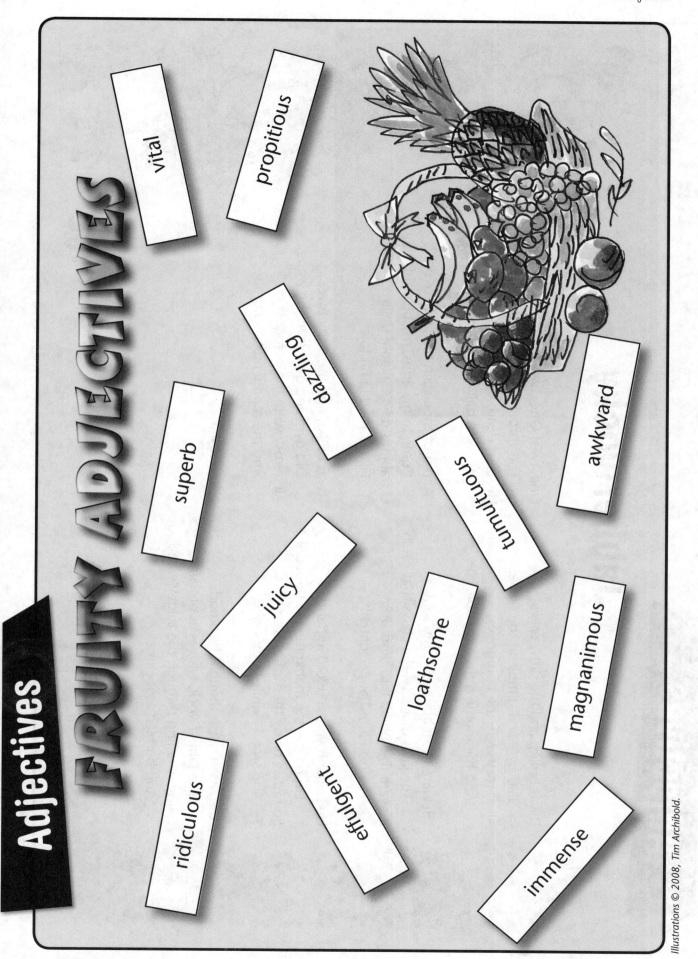

vital

propitious

dazzling

superb

awkward

tumultuous

juicy

loathsome

magnanimous

ridiculous

effulgent

immense

Illustrations © 2008, Tim Archibold.

Adjectives

Jabberwocky

'Twas brillig, and the slithy toves
Did gyre and gimble in the wabe:
All mimsy were the borogoves,
And the mome raths outgrabe.

"Beware the Jabberwock, my son!
The jaws that bite, the claws that catch!
Beware the Jubjub bird, and shun
The frumious Bandersnatch!"

He took his vorpal sword in hand:
Long time the manxome foe he sought –
So rested he by the Tumtum tree,
And stood awhile in thought.

And, as in uffish thought he stood,
The Jabberwock, with eyes of flame,
Came whiffling through the tulgey wood,
And burbled as it came!

One, two! One, two! And through and through
The vorpal blade went snicker-snack!
He left it dead, and with its head
He went galumphing back.

"And hast thou slain the Jabberwock?
Come to my arms, my beamish boy!
O frabjous day! Callooh! Callay!"
He chortled in his joy.

'Twas brillig, and the slithy toves
Did gyre and gimble in the wabe:
All mimsy were the borogoves,
And the mome raths outgrabe.

by Lewis Carroll

Illustrations © 2008, Tim Archibold.

Adjectives

Objective

Revise and extend understanding of adjectives.

Background knowledge

An adjective is a word that describes or modifies a noun. Among other things, it can describe the shape, size or appearance of a noun. For example:

A square box.

The box is big.

A scruffy box.

Nouns can also be described by adjectival phrases. These are groups of words that describe a noun:

A perfectly square box.

The box is bigger than the ball.

A box as scruffy as me.

In each noun phrase there is a headword, an adjective around which the other words are organised.

Activities

This section should involve revision of introductory work on adjectives in Year 3 (see the Year 3 book in the Scholastic Literacy Skills: Grammar and Punctuation series). The activities are extended to include the use of adjectival phrases. As the children set about the task of observing adjectives in a variety of contexts, they need to focus on looking for the descriptive word (or words) and the thing that is being described. In some cases the noun is implicit, as when the back-cover blurb of a book reads brilliant from start to finish. It is actually referring to the book but the noun is, in such cases, not included.

● **Photocopiable page 36 'Choose your adjective'**
As a way of revising the use of adjectives, this activity asks the children to link adjectives to nouns. They can experiment with various combinations, producing unusual and interesting results in some cases. It is also useful to look at which combinations strike them as unacceptable (and why). How many of the adjectives sit comfortably before the nouns? Which ones don't? Encourage the children to share their findings.

● **Photocopiable page 37 'Adjectival phrases'**
The task in this activity is to isolate the string of words

that is acting as an adjectival phrase and, within it, the headword adjective. Explain that the question What is being described? underpins the process of finding the adjectival phrase.

● **Photocopiable page 38 'Match report'**
For this activity, the children will need access to a range of newspapers. It will have an obvious relevance if reports of a recent and important game can be circulated.

Further ideas

● **An adjective beginning with…:** To play this game, the children will need ten cards with ten different letters written on them. Shuffle the cards and place them in a pile, face down. Then say: Think of an adjective that describes…, inserting a noun. It could be a place, a famous person, a television programme, an event in school – any appropriate noun. Having said this, add beginning with and turn over the first card to show its letter. The children then have to come up with an adjective as quickly as they can.

● **Why those quotes?:** The children can collect examples of blurbs on the back covers of books and compare them, asking each other why those particular quotes were used. Why not have one that is less than complimentary? Are the quotes repetitive? How do they affect the reader?

● **Making blurbs:** Provide the children with a current review of a particular children's book, taken from a newspaper or a magazine. Ask them to pinpoint the snippet of text they would print on the back of the book if they were marketing it. Give them a word limit for each short piece of text. Alternatively, they could agree on an optimum number themselves by referring to a copy of photocopiable page 53 'Back cover quotes'.

What's on the CD-ROM

On the CD-ROM you will find:
● Printable versions of all three photocopiable pages.
● Answers to 'Adjectival phrases'.
● Interactive versions of 'Choose your adjective' and 'Adjectival phrases'.

Name:

Adjectives

Choose your adjective

Here's a pile of adjectives:

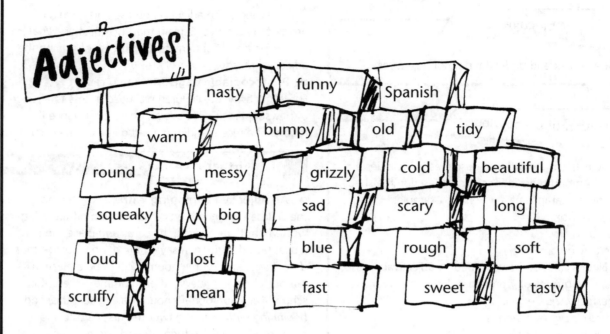

and here's a pile of nouns:

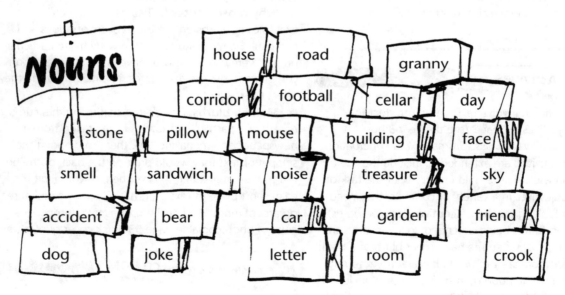

■ Combine 20 of the nouns with suitable adjectives. Write them down on a separate sheet of paper. For example:

messy   house

Illustrations © 1999, Tim Archibold.

Adjectives

Adjectival phrases

An adjectival phrase is a string of words that describes a noun.

| School is | totally brilliant. |

Adjectival phrases stand in place of single adjectives.

| School is brilliant. |

Adjectival phrases contain an adjective.

| School is | totally brilliant. |

■ Look at the text in the speech bubbles. In each one find the string of words that is describing the noun. Underline the string of words. Circle the noun being described.

This picnic is more than enough.

My brother has grown to be bigger than me.

She gave me the sweetest, loveliest, dreamiest smile.

The long and winding road leads to the house.

The letter must be lost in the post.

The weather today is hotter than July.

Nothing beats sailing the big, bright, blue sea.

This football is flat as a pancake.

Illustrations © 1999, Tim Archibold.

■SCHOLASTIC
www.scholastic.co.uk PHOTOCOPIABLE Scholastic Literacy Skills
Grammar and punctuation: Year 4 37

Name:

Adjectives

Match report

■ Football reports use some incredible adjectives. Look at this extract and find some examples. Write the adjective and noun it describes in the table below.

Christian Vieri… is a striker who has blasted into this World Cup with a ready supply of goals in his boots. A solitary deadly strike, his fifth of the tournament, shot Italy into the quarter finals. Once the deed was done the reliable, impenetrable defence clicked the lock shut… It was the mighty attacking presence of Vieri who looked the most dangerous force on the field.

© The Observer (28 June 1998)

Adjective(s)	Noun it describes
mighty, attacking	presence

Adjective(s)	Noun it describes

Text © 1998, Guardian News and Media Ltd; Illustrations © 1999, Tim Archibold.

Similes

Objective

Understand the use of adjectives in figurative language.

Background knowledge

There are many ways in which the English language can provide users with material for finding figurative ways of saying something. The simile involves the direct linkage of one thing with another thing: the link lies in the similarity between the two. These figurative uses can eventually become fossilised into the language (for example, although a coot isn't actually bald, the expression *bald as a coot* has such a currency that people ignore the actual appearance of the bird's head).

Similes differ from metaphors. In a metaphor there is also the likening of one thing to another thing, such as the description of a noisy classroom in terms normally associated with a zoo. However, in similes the direct relation is indicated by the words 'as' or 'like' – for example, *dry like the desert* or *thick as a brick*.

Activities

Similes can provide children with a clear introduction to the use of figurative language. They can discern the connection between what is being described and what it is being likened to – that is, the term used. In the first two activities it is this connection that is the focus. The third activity encourages linguistic investigation, looking at some descriptive terms that need studying to seek out their origins.

● **Photocopiable page 40 'Match the simile'**
Make an enlarged copy of the sheet for the initial stage of this activity. After you have introduced the idea of similes, point out the gap in the first sentence. The children need to ask themselves: *Which adjective can link the two parts of the sentence?* Explain that

this linking is how similes extend the description of something. Go through the next sentence, finding its missing simile as a class, before the children complete the sheet individually or in groups.

● **Photocopiable page 41 'Descriptive similes'**
This activity builds on the previous one by asking the children to devise some examples of similes of their own, one for each of their chosen subjects.

● **Photocopiable page 42 'Old similes'**
Encourage the children to read the information given for each noun. Then they will be able to work out the correct words to complete the similes.

Further ideas

● **Simile collecting:** Once they have been introduced to the concept of similes, children will often give examples of ones they hear used by adults around them. This can be extended by asking the children to make a list of similes at home. They can interview any adults and try making a list of ten. On returning to school, lists can be compared to find common ones and ones unique to their family.
● **Literary similes:** Ask the children to look out for examples of similes in stories and poems they are reading.
● **Modern similes:** The children can look at some of the cultural and historical references in old similes and try to devise their own new ones. Point out that, within a few years, these will also be dated! Which name could they put in place of Croesus in 'as rich as Croesus'? They can use names from the contemporary worlds of business, pop, film and sport.

What's on the CD-ROM

On the CD-ROM you will find:
● Printable versions of all three photocopiable pages.
● Answers to 'Match the simile' and 'Old similes'.
● Interactive versions of 'Match the simile' and 'Old similes'.

Name:

Similes

Match the simile

Similes can be used to describe nouns. They link a description of something to a similar thing.

as slow as a snail

The words **as** and **like** are often used to make a simile. For example:
You're as daft as a brush.
He's as cool as a cucumber.

■ Look at these broken similes. Choose the correct words from the selection at the foot of the page and write them in the spaces provided.

A spring morning is		as a daisy.
The morning went by		as a racing car.
Our teacher was		like a clown.
My brother is		like a giant.
Our baby is		like a kitten.
The secretary is		as a bee.
Your answers were		as a knife.
The classroom was		as a graveyard.
The children were		as a herd of elephants.
The joke fell		as a pancake.

{ as fast }   { as noisy }   { tall }   { playful }   { as sharp }

{ cheerful }   { as quiet }   { as flat }   { as fresh }   { as busy }

PHOTOCOPIABLE   ◼SCHOLASTIC
www.scholastic.co.uk

Similes

Descriptive similes

Simile maker

Think of the thing you're describing.

Think of a quality about it or a descriptive word for it.

Think of something that shares this quality.

Link the two together – you could use the words **as** or **like**.

■ Here are some subjects.

■ Pick **fifteen** and create a simile for each of them.

My friend

Playtimes

The classroom

Football

Assembly

School dinner   The park

Cycling

Swimming

English

Granddad

The news

The supermarket

Maths

My favourite
chocolate bar

A bus journey

The weather today

A bully

My bedroom

Home

Snails

School

Waking up

Salad

SCHOLASTIC
www.scholastic.co.uk   **PHOTOCOPIABLE**   Scholastic Literacy Skills
Grammar and punctuation: Year 4   **41**

Name:

Similes

Old simiLes

■ Look at these old similes. The missing words could be any of the nouns listed in the table. To help you, a is included with each one, explaining its origin.

wise as _____   thin as _____

cool as _____   rich as _____

dead as _____   mad as _____

bald as _____   sure as _____

sour as _____   plain as _____

patient as _____   limp as _____

a coot A coot is a bird whose white bill extends to make a shield over its head.	**Croesus** Croesus was an ancient king said to have great wealth.
vinegar Have you ever drunk a little bit of vinegar? What does it taste like?	**a March hare** During the month of March, mating hares exhibit strange, crazy behaviour.
Solomon Solomon was a king in the Bible who had the gift of great wisdom.	**a glove** How does a glove change when you take your hand out?
Job In the Bible, Job went through terrible times but remained faithful and thoughtful.	**a pikestaff** A pikestaff was a long pole with a spear tip, sometimes measuring 16 feet and hard to conceal.
a dodo Dodos were a species of bird which became extinct in the late 17th century.	**a lath** A long, slim piece of wood, only about 2–3cm wide, used in fences and as a support for slates.
death and taxes These are two things many people would rather avoid, but are pretty sure to face.	**a cucumber** On a warm day the centre of a cucumber has a lower temperature than the air around it.

Intensity

Objective

Learn the degrees of intensity that adjectives can denote.

Background knowledge

A sentence involves a combination of words. There is a process of selection involved in the use of the individual words. One of the finer points of this process of selection concerns the intensity of the adjectives.

If someone spills a drop of tea on the tablecloth, they may say, *Oh, that's annoying*, but they would be exaggerating if they deemed it *completely disastrous*. Adjectives have links with other adjectives, and some of them are more extreme than others.

Activities

These activities deal with convention in the use of adjectives, so there will be an element of subjective judgement. Many people will consider the word *disastrous* to be more extreme than *irritating* on the scale of describing the unpleasantness of something. However, language changes and, within families or groups of friends, certain terms can take on a currency of their own.

● **Photocopiable page 44 'Ordering adjectives'**
This activity looks at the way adjectives can be compared with each other when focusing on a particular quality, such as the brightness of a light (*dim, bright, dazzling, blinding*). The children might be able to think of other adjectives that are similar to the ones given in a particular row and slot them in so that they are in their correct positions within the scale (for example, the word *warm* could be placed in between *cold* and *hot* in the first row).

● **Photocopiable page 45 'Adjective links'**
An essential part of the process of selecting the appropriate adjective in a particular context is the stock of words the speaker or writer has to call upon. This activity encourages children to look at the variety of

adjectives that can be linked to a particular context. The easiest way for the children to carry it out is to start with one adjective, link it to a noun and then find other words that can be substituted for their initial adjective.

● **Photocopiable page 46 'Your intensity scale'**
The intensity of adjectives used to describe something like a spider will vary according to the person making the description. This activity asks the children to explore the varying intensity of their responses to different things. They can use their completed photocopiable page 45 'Adjective links' to provide material for it.

Further ideas

● **'Hot and cold':** Adapt the old game in which people would hide something in a room and, as someone else looked for it, guide them as to how close they were by saying 'Cold… cool… warmer…'. The game relied upon variable temperature as a guide to how close the seeker was to the hidden object. The same game can be played using other scales of intensity, such as those used for happiness and sadness, or fear and confidence.

● **Thesauruses:** The activity on photocopiable page 45 can be extended to include the use of thesauruses. Encourage the children to find new and unfamiliar adjectives.

● **Compare the scale:** Ask the children to look at their comparisons of intensity on their completed copies of photocopiable page 46, and to write the nouns on one set of cards and the adjectives on another. Can their friends match up the cards? Do they match the adjectives to the nouns in the same way? Let the children record the results, with the aim of finding out if there are particular cards that are always chosen as a matching set, evoking the same response.

What's on the CD-ROM

On the CD-ROM you will find:
● Printable versions of all three photocopiable pages.
● Answers to 'Ordering adjectives'.
● Interactive version of 'Ordering adjectives'.

Name:

Intensity

Ordering adjectives

■ Can you sort the adjectives so that the words are in the correct order in each row? The sentences on the left-hand side of the page provide a context.

■ Cut them out and place them in order from one extreme to the other. For example: The first row contains words that are all about temperature. You could arrange them like this – from hottest to coldest:

| boiling | cold | hot | freezing |

a…day	cold	boiling	freezing	hot
feeling…	happy	overjoyed	miserable	sad
a…door	closed	open	ajar	wide open
feeling…	cross	angry	calm	furious
a…landscape	hilly	rolling	flat	mountainous
a…bike	sluggish	speedy	fast	slow
a…person	big	huge	tiny	small
a…light	dim	blinding	bright	dazzling

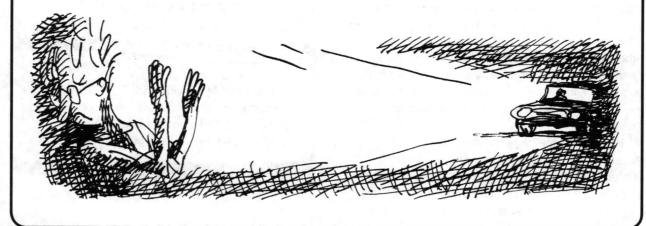

PHOTOCOPIABLE

SCHOLASTIC
www.scholastic.co.uk

Illustrations © 1999, Tim Archibold.

Intensity

Adjective links

■ Collect together similar sets of adjectives. Try to get **five** or more adjectives in each set. For example:

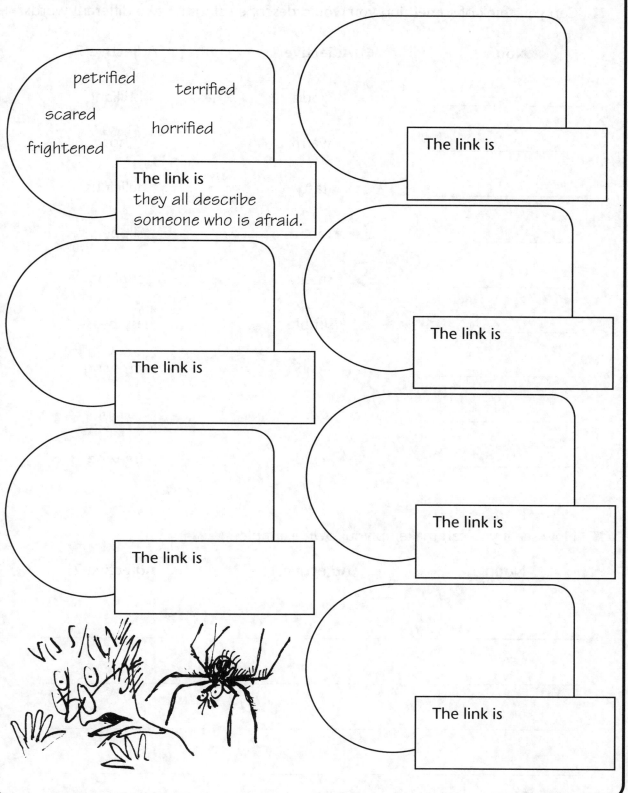

petrified

terrified

scared

horrified

frightened

The link is
they all describe
someone who is afraid.

The link is

The link is

The link is

The link is

The link is

The link is

The link is

Name:

Intensity

Your intensity scale

■ Each row shows two adjectives. They move from the less intense to the more intense.

■ Can you think of something you would describe using the two different words?

Noun	Adjective 1	Adjective 2
_____	good	brilliant
_____	warm	hot
_____	tasty	delicious
_____	smooth	slippery
_____	smelly	stinking
_____	simple	easy peasy
_____	scary	terrifying
_____	quiet	silent
_____	cold	freezing

■ Now see if you can make up your own examples.

Noun	Adjective 1	Adjective 2
_____	_____	_____
_____	_____	_____
_____	_____	_____
_____	_____	_____

PHOTOCOPIABLE

Comparative and superlative

Objective

Understand and use comparative and superlative adjectives.

Background knowledge

Adjectives can indicate the degree to which a noun possesses a particular quality. This is done by using three different forms of adjective:

● **Nominative:** is the plain form of the adjective indicating the quality of a noun (for example, *This tree is tall*).

● **Comparative:** implies a comparison between a noun and another noun or nouns (*This tree is taller*).

● **Superlative:** is an adjective indicating that its noun is the extreme example of a particular quality (*This tree is tallest*).

There are various ways of making the nominative form comparative and superlative:

● **Adding 'er':** 'er' added to the nominative makes the comparative: *big* ➜ *bigger*

● **Adding 'est':** 'est' added to the nominative makes the superlative: *big* ➜ *biggest*

● **Adjectives ending in 'y':** the 'y' is changed to 'i' before the additions are made.

pretty ➜ *prettier* ➜ *prettiest*

● **Longer adjectives:** tend to use 'more' and 'most' to make the comparative and superlative:

beautiful ➜ *more beautiful* ➜ *most beautiful*

● **There are some exceptions:** for example:

good ➜ *better* ➜ *best*

bad ➜ *worse* ➜ *worst*

Activities

Children like latching on to big words. The terminology used in these activities is appealing to them because even though it is fairly easy to find, identify and create examples of the three types of adjective, they have these marvellous terms – nominative, comparative, superlative – attached to them! Children can learn the trio of terms almost like a rhyme.

● **Photocopiable page 48 'Nominative, comparative, superlative'**

This activity asks the children to sort the adjectives into the three varying degrees (it links to photocopiable page 44 'Ordering adjectives', which introduced children to the idea of sorting adjectives in a general way).

● **Photocopiable page 49 'Varieties of comparison'**

One rule for deciding whether to alter the endings or use 'more' or 'most' is to count the syllables: one-syllable adjectives tend to use 'er' and 'est'; two-syllable adjectives can do either; three-syllable adjectives tend to use 'more' and 'most'.

● **Photocopiable page 50 'Ordering by degree'**

As a reinforcement activity, this task involves the children in devising trios of nouns to fit trios of adjectives.

Further ideas

● **Characters:** Ask the children to think of adjectives that can be used to describe personalities and to make a comparative trio for each adjective.

● **Bidding:** Ask the children to think of something that can be described by using a particular adjective (such as a 'silly' cartoon). Explain that they then have to think of comparative examples. Working with the adjective 'miserable', for example, they may decide that a cold day is 'miserable' and that playtime on a cold day is 'more miserable'. They can record their examples until they have a scale of progress.

● **Records:** Books like *Guinness World Records* can be referred to for examples of recognised superlatives. Ask the children to think of an adjective and use their referencing skills to see if there are any records for the adjective in its superlative form.

What's on the CD-ROM

On the CD-ROM you will find:

● Printable versions of all three photocopiable pages.

● Answers to 'Nominative, comparative, superlative' and 'Varieties of comparison'.

● Interactive version of 'Nominative, comparative, superlative'.

Name:

Nominative, comparative, superlative

An adjective can have three degrees:

There is the plain adjective, sometimes called the **nominative**,

the adjective that compares, the **comparative**

and the adjective that beats them all, the **superlative**.

I am short.

I am shorter

I am shortest.

■ Write out these adjectives, sorting them into order – nominative, comparative and superlative.

tallest   tall   taller

smart   smarter   smartest

happiest   happier   happy

cool   coolest   cooler

juicy   juiciest   juicer

thin   thinnest   thinner

hotter   hot   hottest

unhappiest   unhappy   unhappier

Illustrations © 1999, Tim Archibold.

Varieties of comparison

The three degrees of adjective can be made by altering the ending of the word:

quiet   quiet**er**   quiet**est**
silly   sill**ier**   sill**iest**

They can also be made with the words **more** and **most**:

quiet   **more** quiet   **most** quiet
silly   **more** silly   **most** silly

There are also trios that don't fit any rule.

good   better   best
bad   worse   worst

> When you make the changes with adjectives ending in **y** you change **y** to **i**.

Beautiful… beautifuller… beautifullest – doesn't sound right.

I tend to say bigger rather than more big.

■   Try the different ways of making the three degrees with these adjectives. Check by seeing if the trio sounds right when you say it.

Nominative	Comparative	Superlative
long		
honest		
small		
dangerous		
young		
old		
different		
sharp		
peaceful		
careful		
brilliant		
tall		

Illustrations © 1999, Tim Archibold.

Name:

Comparative and superlative

Ordering by degree

■ Fill in the boxes with trios of nouns that fit the adjectives.
For example:

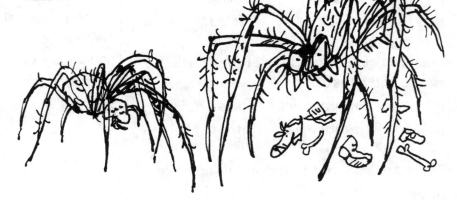

A spider	is scary	A kid-eating spider	is scarier	A kid-eating poisonous spider	is scariest
	is scary		is scarier		is scariest
	is good		is better		is best
	is fast		is faster		is fastest
	is big		is bigger		is biggest
	is dangerous		is more dangerous		is most dangerous
	is tasty		is tastier		is tastiest

Illustrations © 1999, Tim Archibold.

PHOTOCOPIABLE

■SCHOLASTIC
www.scholastic.co.uk

Developing adjectives

Objective

Develop the use of adjectives in writing.

Writing focus

These writing activities focus on the use of adjectives, with particular reference to their use in certain types of writing.

Skills to writing

● **Connections with nouns**

Grasping the use of adjectives is a two-way process. It's not enough just to learn the meaning of adjectives, they need to be learned in connection with nouns. Children need to develop the habit of working from noun to adjective and adjective to noun. Looking at familiar nouns, they should be encouraged to consider the adjectives that could be used to describe them. Similarly, as they encounter new adjectives they need to consider to which nouns they could be applied.

● **Phrases**

Gather adjectival phrases. It's surprising how common these are – but given the inclusion of similes, imagery and qualified adjectives like *utterly disgusting*, the list ends up being quite extensive and containing some of the best examples children will want to use.

● **Text types**

Keep an eye on the way certain types of adjective appear in certain types of text. The football example on photocopiable page 38 'Match report' is just one way in which a particular area of language use has acquired its own terminology. Children can listen and look out for other uses in other contexts. For example, are certain adjectives particular to dance contests, car programmes or mystery stories?

● **Report texts**

Adjectives have a useful role to play in the planning and writing of report texts. Children will often write the base facts in their reports and one way of enriching these is to ask them to read through each others' drafts, checking to see whether they can effectively envisage the subject matter. Is there a need for more description?

● **Persuasive adjectives**

Adjectives have a different role to play in persuasive speaking and writing. Whereas a report text will generally aim for a neutral description of a subject, persuasion is out to influence the reader. As a result advertisements, letters to the newspaper, protest leaflets and so on, will usually include stronger descriptions of whatever they are promoting and sometimes derogatory descriptions of the alternative.

● **Characterisation**

Characterisation is the means whereby writers present their characters to the reader. Adjectives play an obvious part in direct characterisation, where the narrator just says *He was horrible* or *She was very brave*. The more subtle type of characterisation is to influence the reader's view of a character by showing us what they looked like (*sinister eyes*) and placing them in a context (*in a dusty classroom, full of old stuffed animals*). As they describe both appearance and context, children need to consider how these will affect the reader's perception of their character.

Activities

● **Photocopiable page 53 'Back cover quotes'**

Book covers often include enthusiastic, adjective-rich endorsements of the product. These examples should act as a starter before the children look at other books to study the adjectival descriptions in the reviews. They could try writing similar quotes for books they know.

● **Photocopiable page 54 'Boasts'**

As children read the boasts and try to write their own, they will need to consider the most extreme ways in which the quality they have chosen could manifest itself. They may even want to perform an enactment of their boasts as a drama activity.

Write on

● Adjective collage

Over time, cut out adjectives from newspapers, adverts, posters and other texts. The children can use these to build up a collage. Ask them to stick any examples they find on a large sheet of paper, building up a collage from the centre outwards. It can stimulate some good discussion at home as to which words are adjectives and what they mean, as children gather examples to bring into school.

● Simile generator

The simile *as tall as a giraffe* probably came about when writers wanted to describe a tall person, but for children to develop similes in their writing it is often easier to work backwards. This involves thinking of objects or names that capture their imagination, such as *asteroid* or *referee*, and then asking what similes they could create from the line *as _____ as an asteroid*. As sudden? As cataclysmic? Encourage the children to keep their best examples for use at a later date.

● Jabber

Children can use 'Jabberwocky' (see poster page 34) as the starting point for their own nonsense verses, in which they create nouns and adjectives. It is not as easy as it first sounds, particularly if they want their text to sound like the feelings it is trying to evoke. The children will need an underlying narrative, such as someone losing and finding a treasure. However, once the treasure is in its nonsense form, it will need an appropriate nonsense adjective.

● Villains

Villains are great fun to create. A good exercise on characterisation is to generate villains. Children can start by listing the top ten villains and consider what it was about Hook's manner or Vader's appearance that made them work so well as a villain. How would they describe the appearance of a Cruella or the Wicked Witch of the West? What about Dracula's castle? How did that enhance his character? Having gathered examples, children can use these to stimulate the construction of, and language used for, their own example.

What's on the CD-ROM

On the CD-ROM you will find:
● Printable versions of both photocopiable pages.

Developing adjectives

Back cover quotes

■ Often the back of a book quotes what reviewers said about it. Look through these examples to find adjectives or adjectival phrases. Circle the ones you find.

'Terry Jones is undoubtedly one of the most consistently entertaining writers for children.'
Books for Your Children

'Fantasy, adventure and morality are perfectly mixed in this funny, fast-moving story. A marvellous book.'
The Good Book Guide to Children's Books

> **NICOBOBINUS**
> BY TERRY JONES

'A truly delightful story… warmly recommended.'
School Librarian

'A lovely book – funny, imaginative and both clever and comforting.'
The Sunday Telegraph

> **HARVEY ANGELL**
> BY DIANA HENDRY

'A hugely entertaining novel.'
The Sunday Telegraph

'Anthony Horowitz has created a scary and unmissable old hag.'
The Sunday Times

> **GRANNY**
> BY ANTHONY HOROWITZ

'…one of the best books I've ever read. It's funny, moving and it handles difficult subjects with skill and great respect.'
Paula Danziger

'A marvellous book – funny and wise.'
Books for Keeps

> **TWO WEEKS WITH THE QUEEN**
> BY MORRIS GLEITZMANN

Name:

Developing adjectives

Boasts

Here are some boasts collected from various people and places:

I know someone who
can run so fast
he meets himself
coming back.

I know someone who's
so good at jumping
she can jump across a
river and back without
touching the other side.

There's a man round here
who is so tall
he has to climb a ladder to shave himself
when he was born he was so big
it was impossible to name all of him at once
he grew so fast
his head grew three inches through the top of
his hat.

Adapted from a collection in *The Kingfisher Book of Children's Poetry* selected by Michael Rosen.

Each one boasts about an adjective:

so fast   so good at jumping   so tall   so big

■ Try making up your own incredible boasts. Start with:

I know someone who is so…

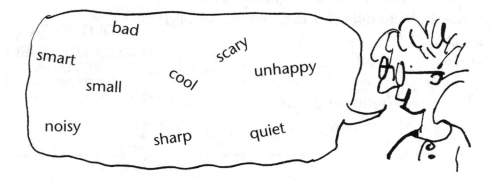

bad
smart
scary
cool
unhappy
small
noisy
sharp
quiet

PHOTOCOPIABLE

SCHOLASTIC
www.scholastic.co.uk

Chapter 3
Apostrophes and hyphens

Introduction

Apostrophes present a real challenge to children learning how and when to use punctuation. In this chapter the first two activities provide a grounding in the types of apostrophe in use. 'Apostrophes in use' and 'Refining punctuation in writing' both connect this work with actual texts. This chapter also explains the different functions of hyphens and dashes.

Poster notes

Apostrophe chart (page 56)

This chart supports 'Apostrophes for possession' by providing a poster version of the rules for the addition of apostrophes to show possession. As a class, collect further examples of the four different categories of the possessive apostrophe and display them on a large sheet next to the poster. Can the children spot all the nouns that are objects of possession? Can they provide further examples?

Contractions (page 57)

This poster lists some words in which the apostrophe is used for contraction. Aside from acting as a reminder and a spelling tool, use this poster to occasionally pick one contraction and ask children what the original two words (or longer word) were, that have now been contracted to this form.

In this chapter

Apostrophes for possession page 58	Identify possessive apostrophes in reading and writing and to whom or what they refer.
Apostrophes for contraction page 62	Distinguish between apostrophes for possession and contraction.
Apostrophes in use page 66	Understand the uses of the apostrophe in reading and writing.
Hyphens and dashes page 70	Identify and begin to understand the use of hyphens and dashes.
Refining punctuation in writing page 74	Consolidate the use of punctuation marks in writing.

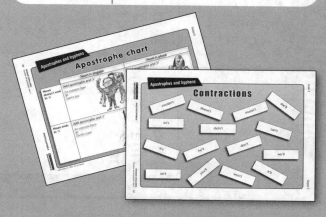

Apostrophes and hyphens

Apostrophe chart

	Noun is singular	Noun is plural
Noun doesn't end in 's'	Add apostrophe and 's' for example: Sam in Sam's dog	Add apostrophe and 's' for example: children in children's dog
Noun ends in 's'	Add apostrophe and 's' for example: Paris in Paris's tower	Add apostrophe for example: babies in babies' rattles

Illustrations © 2008, Tim Archibold.

Scholastic Literacy Skills
Grammar and punctuation: Year 4

PHOTOCOPIABLE

SCHOLASTIC
www.scholastic.co.uk

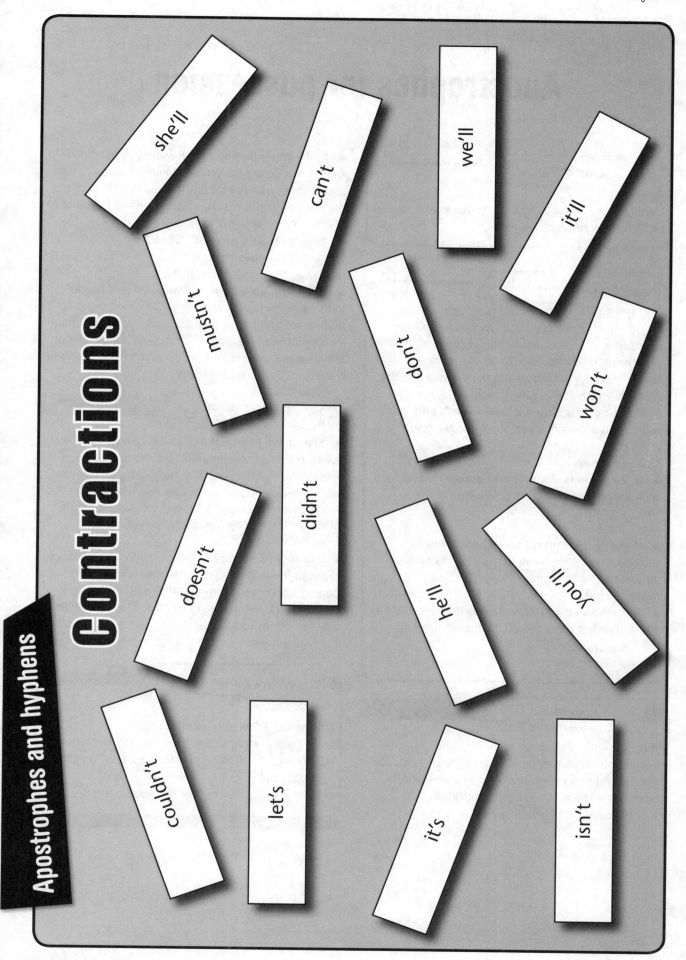

Contorections

Apostrophes and hyphens

she'll

can't

we'll

it'll

mustn't

don't

won't

doesn't

didn't

he'll

you'll

couldn't

let's

it's

isn't

Apostrophes for possession

Objective

Identify possessive apostrophes in reading and writing and to whom or what they refer.

Background knowledge

Apostrophes can be used to show possession. An apostrophe in a word that is a noun can show it possesses a following item (for example, 'Sean's book'). Rules for adding apostrophes depend on the nouns to which they are being added.

- **If the noun is singular and doesn't end in 's':** you add an apostrophe and an 's', for example:
Sam's dog
Kate's football
- **If the noun is singular and ends in 's':** you add an apostrophe and an 's', for example:
Ross's cat
Paris's tower
- **If the noun is plural and doesn't end in 's':** you add an apostrophe and an 's', for example:
the children's dog
the mice's nest
- **If the noun is plural and ends in 's':** you add an apostrophe but don't add an 's', for example:
the babies' rattles
the teachers' mugs

Activities

When learning punctuation rules like these, the most effective introduction is for children to have access to the rules and to try them out on a variety of words and phrases. The activities here ask children to look at various examples of the different rules.

- **Photocopiable page 59 'Reading apostrophes'**
As an introductory example, children are asked to read some sentences and examine the relationship between the word that contains the apostrophe and the word which is the object of possession.
- **Photocopiable page 60 'Our lists'**
This activity involves children in the task of making lists of phrases that include apostrophes.
- **Photocopiable page 61 'Singular and plural'**
In this activity children encounter the various rules for adding apostrophes of possession to nouns. They then try a set of examples. The two crucial questions about the noun are: *Is it singular or plural?* and *Does it end in the letter 's'?* (see poster page 56).

Further ideas

- **Examples:** Provide the children with reading material in which they can find examples of the possessive apostrophe that cover each of the rules. Can they think of their own examples of phrases that use apostrophes for possession? Suggest that they compile examples which are inspired by characters from books or television.
- **Examining examples:** When children find examples of apostrophes used to indicate possession in their reading, encourage them to use photocopiable page 59 'Reading apostrophes' to examine the relationship between the word with the apostrophe and the noun to which it belongs.

 ## What's on the CD-ROM

On the CD-ROM you will find:
- Printable versions of all three photocopiable pages.
- Answers to 'Reading apostrophes' and 'Singular and plural'.
- Interactive version of 'Reading apostrophes'.

Reading apostrophes

■ Look at these sentences. In each there is a word with a possessive apostrophe. Something belongs to the noun that ends with the apostrophe.

Look at Sam's dog.

The apostrophe shows:

The dog belongs to Sam.

■ Complete the sentences, showing who or what 'possesses' something.

Sophie's bike is really fast.

The _____ belongs to _____.

Mr Hall repaired the guitar's string.

The _____ belongs to _____.

Maya collected each class's register.

The _____ belongs to _____.

We found a stripy snail's shell.

The _____ belongs to _____.

Everyone waited for the orchestra's conductor.

The _____ belongs to _____.

The farmer put the cows' food in their trough.

The _____ belongs to _____.

After school, Micah and Louie went to Toby's house.

The _____ belongs to _____.

Illustrations © 1999, Tim Archibold.

Apostrophes for possession

Our lists

■ Jamie asked eight children in his class: *What is your favourite toy?* He recorded the results using apostrophes to show who said what.

Tracy's football

Kirpan's magic set

Caroline's troll

Jan's train set

Harry's space rider

Tara's chemistry set

Kyle's yo-yo

Nathan's computer game

■ Ask children in your class each question and make a list under each heading. Remember to use the apostrophe.

Best toy	Clothing	Relative who gets the most visits
Which toy is your absolute favourite?	What's your favourite item of clothing?	Which of your relatives do you visit the most?

Apostrophes for possession

Singular and plural

Where you place an apostrophe depends on the word it is added to.

The owner	The rule	Examples
is singular, doesn't end in 's'	add an apostrophe and 's'	Sam's dog Kate's football
is singular, ends in 's'	add an apostrophe and 's'	Ross's cat Paris's tower
is plural, doesn't end in 's'	add an apostrophe and 's'	the children's dog the mice's nest
is plural, ends in 's'	add an apostrophe only (no 's')	the babies' rattles the teachers' mugs

Look at this sentence.

The bike belongs to Pete.

Turn it into a phrase that

has an apostrophe. It becomes:

Pete's bike

Look at the thing or person who owns. Is there one or more? Does the word end in 's'?

■ Turn these sentences into phrases that have apostrophes.

The football belongs to Kate. _____

The quiz game belongs to the class. _____

The playground belongs to the children. _____

The mugs belong to the teachers. _____

The lids belong to the boxes. _____

The houses belong to the people. _____

The farm belongs to the women. _____

The driver belongs to the bus. _____

The cat belongs to Ross. _____

Illustrations © 1999, Tim Archibold.

Apostrophes for contraction

Objective

Distinguish between apostrophes for possession and contraction.

Background knowledge

Apostrophes can mark possession but they can also mark the contraction of a word or words. They show where two words have been contracted together with some of the letters removed, marking the point at which the letters once stood – so 'did not', for example, loses the 'o' to become 'didn't'.

In many cases the apostrophe marks a contraction of words that we would not now use. People tend not to say 'I did not…' unless it's for emphasis. We usually say 'I didn't…' In 'o'clock' the apostrophe marks a contraction of a phrase ('of the clock') that has dropped out of common usage.

There is an ongoing development of the apostrophe's use, such that it now features in contractions like 'should've' and 'must've'. These contractions are not favoured in some quarters but it remains to be seen whether they stick around.

Activities

As the children come across an apostrophe they can look to see if it is marking contraction or possession. They then need to ask, if it is an apostrophe of possession, *What belongs to whom?* If it is an apostrophe of contraction they can try to identify the words that are being contracted (the words that are 'behind' the phrase that is apostrophised).

● **Photocopiable page 63 'Contraction'**
By matching the two sets of words, children are able to look at some of the common contractions and the words they contract.

● **Photocopiable page 64 'Contraction or possession?'**
This activity asks children to identify examples of apostrophes used for contraction and those used for possession. Each word containing an apostrophe is highlighted so that the children can see at a glance which words they should focus on. As they classify the apostrophes, remind them to consider the key points mentioned above regarding the difference between an apostrophe of possession and one of contraction.

● **Photocopiable page 65 'Sort the apostrophes'**
The story contains 17 apostrophes – eight of possession, nine of contraction. As the children find them, they can record them using formats they will be familiar with from earlier activities.

Further ideas

● **Contraction detecting:** Ask the children to record a conversation and listen for the contractions in their speech when they play it back. Ask them to record a five-minute discussion about a theme with which they are all familiar and on which they all have opinions. They can then play back the tape as many times as they need to, stopping and noting down any contractions in their speech.

● **Varied contractions:** Ask the children to list any new contractions they encounter in their reading or in their everyday conversations. It is likely that there will be a number of contemporary or localised contractions they will use in speech, such as *ain't*, *tha's kiddin'*.

What's on the CD-ROM

On the CD-ROM you will find:
● Printable versions of all three photocopiable pages.
● Answers to 'Contraction' and 'Contraction or possession?'.
● Interactive version of 'Contraction or possession?'.

Apostrophes for contraction

Contraction

Apostrophes are used to contract words together. This means that we can write them down in the way we say them.

Instead of saying
  Lola ate the cake she had made,
people often say
  Lola ate the cake she'd made.

All of it?

When we write this we use the apostrophe.
It shows where something has been removed.

Lola ate the cake she ↓ d made.   Lola ate the cake she'd made.
                      ha

■ Write the contractions alongside the original phrases.

we will _____
he will _____
does not _____
it is _____
he would _____
have not _____
is not _____
cannot _____
let us _____
do not _____
did not _____
you will _____
you are _____
we have _____
she would _____
must not _____
she will _____
I will _____
I am _____
could not _____

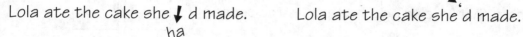

couldn't   can't   mustn't

she'd   didn't   you're

doesn't   we'll   let's

she'll   don't

he'd   haven't
        I'm
                he'll
I'll   isn't

                you'll
we've   it's

Illustrations © 1999, Tim Archibold.

**Apostrophes
for contraction**

Contraction or possession?

■ Look at the sentences. Sort them into two groups. Put a 'P' in the box for a sentence that has an apostrophe of possession. Put a 'C' in the box for a sentence that has an apostrophe of contraction. The words have been circled to help you.

Chris (can't) remember his house in Scotland. ☐

(Chris's) family come from Scotland. ☐

(Don't) put too much food in the fish tank. ☐

(I'll) check that (we've) closed the classroom door. ☐ ☐

I think (I'll) go to the park after school. ☐

My class (hasn't) done PE this week. ☐

My grandpa said (he'd) meet me from school. ☐

On (Mum's) birthday we made her a cake. ☐

Some people are painting the (doctor's) surgery. ☐

The cook made the (children's) dinners. ☐

The farmer sheared the (sheep's) wool. ☐

The plug on the hoover (didn't) work. ☐

Illustrations © 1999, Tim Archibold.

Apostrophes for contraction

Sort the apostrophes

■ Look at this piece of writing and find the apostrophes of possession and the apostrophes of contraction. List them on a separate sheet of paper, and show how they work:

For an apostrophe of possession, write

the _____ of the _____

(for example, *the journey of the sheep*)

For an apostrophe of contraction, write
the full form of the word after the contraction

(for example, *he'd – he would*)

One day a shepherd thought he'd take his sheep to a new, green hillside. The sheep's journey took them down some difficult paths. One little lamb couldn't keep up. The shepherd didn't see a wolf sneak up and grab her. The wolf was about to eat her when the lamb noticed the wolf's whistle in his pocket.

"Oh you mustn't eat me," she said. "I can't die without a send-off."

The wolf was puzzled.

"Please play your whistle," she said. "I'll do a little dance for my funeral and then you'll eat me."

Even more puzzled, the wolf agreed to the lamb's request.

He played and the lamb danced, but the shepherd heard the wolf's music. He sent his fierce dogs. As the shepherd's dogs chased him away the wolf realised the lamb's trick.

"That'll teach me a lesson," he said. "I've been tricked into doing a musician's job instead of a wolf's."

Based on a fable by Aesop

Apostrophes in use

Objective

Understand the uses of the apostrophe in reading and writing.

Background knowledge

The apostrophe enjoys a varied usage. It joined the English language from French in the 16th century and its usage spread from contraction to possession. It now gets overused, sometimes being inserted before any '-s' ending (for example, 'pop and crisp's', 'Carpet's at bargain prices'). At the other extreme it has dropped out of usage in many contexts, deemed to be unnecessary as the job it would be doing can often be gauged from the context in which it would be used. This can be seen in product logos and signs. It features on Cadbury's products and in the name Waterstone's, but not on Levis jeans, for example.

Activities

These activities present materials in which children look closely at how apostrophes are used. An important way in which children will develop their understanding of this punctuation mark is by undertaking the process of reading texts that contain examples of apostrophes, followed by reviewing where they could have used them in their own writing.

- **Photocopiable page 67 'Santa Fe'**
This complicated poem is made comprehensible by its apostrophes. The children are asked to make sense of the action in the fourth, fifth and sixth stanzas. One way of doing this would be to write the characters' names – Cook, Turkey and Jelly – next to the ones the poet uses. They can then figure out who is eating whom!

- **Photocopiable page 68 'Redrafting'**
It is crucial that this redrafting activity is not seen as an end in itself. It should act as a starter only, with children getting into the habit of looking at their use of apostrophes when they redraft their work generally.

- **Photocopiable page 69 'Usage survey'**
Starting with names of restaurants, the children are asked to look at the usage of the apostrophe. This involves them in an aspect of language that is undergoing change, as the apostrophe drifts out of use in a number of contexts. Let the activity lead in to a discussion of the usefulness of the apostrophe.

Further ideas

- **Redrafting:** Children can review pieces of their own writing, finding points at which they could have used apostrophes.
- **Uses around us:** Ask the children to look out for uses of the apostrophe on shop signs and notices. They may notice examples of the apostrophe misused.
- **Phone-book doubles:** Children can scan the phone book for examples of businesses with identical names, bar the apostrophe. Two businesses called Paulines may be listed, but one may be 'Pauline's' and the other 'Paulines'. They could do some investigative reporting into how companies become listed in the phone book and what checking process there is over punctuation, perhaps speaking to local businesses about their use of the apostrophe in their business names. The variety of ways in which the apostrophe is used in everyday language offers children a chance to look at the creation and establishment of a convention – rather than just learning the rules that govern its use!

What's on the CD-ROM

On the CD-ROM you will find:
- Printable versions of all three photocopiable pages.
- Answers to 'Redrafting'.
- Interactive version of 'Redrafting'.

Apostrophes in use

Santa Fe

■ Look at the poem. Try to work out what is happening. Write notes alongside stanzas 4, 5 and 6.

It was a stormy night
one Christmas day
as they fell awake
on the Santa Fe

Three clues:
the 'Hobbler' is the cook,
the 'Gobbler' is the turkey,
the 'Wobbler' is the jelly.

Turkey, jelly
and the ship's old cook
all jumped out
of a recipe book

The jelly wobbled
the turkey gobbled
and after them both
the old cook hobbled

Gobbler gobbled
Hobbler's Wobbler.
Hobbler gobbled
Wobbler's Gobbler.

Gobbly-gobbler
gobbled Wobbly
Hobbly-hobbler
Gobbled Gobbly.

Gobbler gobbled
Hobble's Wobble
Hobble gobbled
gobbled Wobble.

gobble gobble
wobble wobble
hobble gobble
wobble gobble

from *Mind Your Own Business* by Michael Rosen

■SCHOLASTIC
www.scholastic.co.uk   **PHOTOCOPIABLE**   **Scholastic Literacy Skills**
Grammar and punctuation: Year 4   **67**

Name:

Apostrophes in use

Redrafting

■ Look at this piece of writing. Check the apostrophes. Are there:
  • singular and plural uses of the apostrophe of possession?
  • apostrophes of contraction in the right place?
  • apostrophes placed only where they are needed?

Yesterday I went to Sams house. I have'nt been there before. Sams brother Chris was there. Hes at college. We played on Chri'ss computer. Hed only had it a week. Then Sam said "Lets' go to the park, so we did.' Our friends were there. We joined in our friends's game, swinging on the playgrounds railings.

We couldnt' stay because Sams mum called us in for tea.

Sam was slurping his soup. His mum said, "Thats disgusting. Dont slurp."

We ate really quickly and Sam said, "Weve got to go out again now."

"No you dont," his Mum said, "its' time for Paul to go home." So we sulked.

■ Write down your corrected version on a separate sheet of paper.

Apostrophes in use

Usage survey

The apostrophe is sometimes used too much.

Or it is not used when it could have been.

■ Photocopy a column of restaurants from the telephone directory. Stick it in the blank column on the right-hand side of this page.

■ Put a circle around the restaurants that name the owner.

How many could have used an apostrophe but don't?

How many do use an apostrophe?

■ Look at other sections of the phone book or at local shop signs and try to find examples of 'left-out' apostrophes.

Illustrations © 1999, Tim Archibold.

Hyphens and dashes

Objective

Identify and begin to understand the use of hyphens and dashes.

Background knowledge

Hyphens and dashes can be used in various ways. Historically there are some obscure rules, particularly those governing the use of the hyphen. The simplest guidance is that hyphens are used to join together two parts of a word into one. So, 'short' and 'sighted' become the single word 'short-sighted'.

The dash is an informal and increasingly common punctuation mark that can be used to insert words that clarify or interject into a sentence, for example:

My gran – who is eighty – plays football.
I looked around and – thankfully – there were my keys.

The dash can also tag bits onto a sentence:
Meet me at four – don't be late.

Dashes are often used instead of other marks such as commas, which could have been used in the first two examples above.

Activities

The distinction between the dash and hyphen is an important one. They perform different functions. Children will be able to find examples of hyphenated words in any texts and will also encounter the dash used in many types of writing.

● **Photocopiable page 71 'Link words'**
This activity plays upon children's familiarity with various words they may not even have realised were hyphenated. In this way it introduces the types of word in which hyphens are used.

● **Photocopiable page 72 'Letter lines'**
The informality of a letter between friends lends itself to the use of the dash. In this example children can look at the text carefully to see where dashes can be inserted.
● **Photocopiable page 73 'Sports day'**
This activity plays with the idea of mock hyphenated words, asking children to construct a list of imaginary activities for a sports day using hyphenated words.

Further ideas

● **Create words:** Children can use the hyphen as a way of creating new words to add to the language. They can start with a simple noun, verb or adjective and see if they can make new words that could make sense.
● **Finding hyphens:** Ask the children to use a dictionary to find various words with hyphens. They can also compare different dictionaries – words will be hyphenated in some but not in others. Explain that over time, hyphenated words can lose their hyphen (for example, 'haystack').
● **Shop words:** Looking through the local directory, the children can find some examples of hyphenated business names. These could include some interesting features of language play (for example 'Toy-u-like' or 'CD-4-U').

What's on the CD-ROM

On the CD-ROM you will find:
● Printable versions of all three photocopiable pages.
● Answers to 'Link words' and 'Letter lines'.
● Interactive versions of 'Link words' and 'Letter lines'.

Hyphens and dashes

Link words

Hyphens can connect compound words together.

■ Look at the two sets of words below. Cut out the different halves of the words and join them up to create hyphenated words.

Sixty- could go with *four*, for example.

clip-	sixty-	open-	sky-	cross-
second-	tell-	roller-	short-	co-

four	minded	section	clop	ordinate
coaster	hand	diving	tale	sighted

Illustrations © 1999, Tim Archibold.

Name:

Hyphens and dashes

Letter lines

Dashes can be used to slot things into sentences. (Commas can be used in a similar way.)

Annie – my sister – starts Nursery today.

Dashes tag things onto sentences:

Don't forget to bring a packed lunch for the trip – no glass bottles!

Dashes are often used to punctuate sentences in informal notes and letters.

I've got to go now – see ya' soon!

■ Here is a letter from one friend to another. Put the dashes where they should go. Each sentence could have one or two.

Dear Jack,

Just a few bits of news not in any order.

We miss you at school come back.

Ms Cooper who is sixty this year is retiring.

She is going to arrange a big party so she says.

Mr Harper our school nurse told me to say "Hello" to you.

I am now the best footballer in our class I think.

Our garden swing the old rusty one is falling down.

My mum is coming home from my gran's can't wait to see her.

Tomorrow it's science my favourite lesson.

On Saturday I'm going to London just for a day.

Got to go now write soon.

Sam

■ Choose four of the sentences and rewrite them on a separate sheet of paper. Explain the jobs that the dashes are doing.

Hyphens and dashes

Sports day

■ Copy the words from the box, arranging them in different orders and putting in hyphens to create some new games for a sports day.
For example: *balance-the-shark*
■ What would the games involve?
■ Could you invent some rules?
■ Write some notes on the back of this sheet.

eat	the	shark
throw	a	teacher
balance	my	elephant
hunt	your	bus
chase	an	egg

The games

Illustrations © 1999, Tim Archibold.

Refining punctuation in writing

Objective

Consolidate the use of punctuation marks in writing.

Writing focus

Through looking at practical, real text examples of the punctuation marks covered in this section, children can be encouraged to use the marks in their own writing.

Skills to writing

● Revising writing

The best resource for encouraging children to use punctuation in their own writing is to see it at use, briefly and often, in common texts. Keep on the lookout for apostrophes and, as they are found, deconstruct them. Are they possession or contraction? If the former, who possesses what? What rule has been applied? If the latter, what has been omitted?

● Newspaper apostrophes

Hunt and define the use of the apostrophe in a range of texts. Give the children two copies of a newspaper and ask them to work in teams to find as many as they can. You could even score it differentially – two points for possession and five for omission – to get them focused on exactly what sort of example they find.

● Checking apostrophes

Apostrophes provide a useful focus for redrafting activities. At this age apostrophes are easily left out or misapplied. Ask the children to revisit some previous pieces of writing with a view to identifying any revisions they could make. Moving beyond their written work, encourage the children to look in the wider environment and at other printed texts for examples of apostrophe omission or error. It's a common one – so they should find a few!

● Contractions

Contracted words can be used to good effect in the writing of dialogue. In narrative dialogue, *do not…* sounds clumsy, where most people would say *don't*. Using the examples listed on photocopiable page 63 'Contraction' the children can give a natural feel to the speech they write.

● Dashing asides

Dashes can be presented as a way of adding an aside – throwaway additions to a sentence. Placing them at the end of a sentence raises the possibility of a quick, additional comment – should anyone want to make it. Overuse would be irritating, but children could consider using this strategy every so often – I mean, why not?

Activities

● Photocopiable page 76 'Imagine'

The various ideas promoted on this photocopiable sheet provide a stimulus for either report writing – presenting a report text on what you would find in a pirate's locker – and eventually for story writing. For a report text, keep to the frame of paragraphs and sentences that pick apart and report on their subject. The advantage of using subject matter like this for report writing is that the children are freed from the constraints of accuracy – they just use their imagination. The possessions could also be used to stimulate story ideas. What's so special about the pirate's locker? What if it was stolen? What if it was lost? What if a child found the locker and the pirate was looking for it?

● Photocopiable page 77 'They said…'

The dialogue starters on this photocopiable sheet pick up on the notion of contracted speech being more appropriate to direct speech. Tell the children to cut out the starters and place them face down on the table. Invite them to select one and devise a speech sentence a character could say that begins with those words. This could be done as part of the process of developing ideas for a story. If, for example, they have devised a story about a pirate losing his locker, why would he say *You mustn't…* Could it be: *Whatever happens, you mustn't look inside?*

Write on

● **Equip characters**

Together, devise characters for an adventure story and kit them out with the possessions they will take on their adventures. Whether it's 'Tex's rope-ladder' or 'Imogen's parachute', the children can decide why that character needs that item. Point out that a character is never kitted out with something they won't use at some point in the story. The gadget, the spell, the piece of junk they found – they all come in useful at some point in the plot.

● **Story titles**

Kit's Wilderness and Uncle Montague's Tales of Terror are two examples of possessive story titles. The children could use the idea as a way of creating interesting story ideas of their own. To add a challenge, why not insist on alliteration. What, for example, might lie behind The Count's Curtain or in The Beefeater's Bin-Bag?

● **Hyphenated names**

Devise some interesting characters using hyphenated names, a bit like the odd games devised on photocopiable page 73 'Sports day'. What sort of character is Soup-Snaffler? A character like Child-Guzzler is obviously one to avoid, but what about Pirate-Teacher? Once they have devised their hyphen names, invite the children to swap characters around and plan out adventures in which one of their characters meets a character devised by another child.

● **Possession poems**

Ask the class to devise some list poems that tell us something about the possessions of well-known characters. Take the birthday parties of certain characters. What would they be like?
At Dracula's birthday party they…
At Captain Hook's birthday party they…
Finish the lines and add some more to create a list poem that catalogues insights into favourite characters.

What's on the CD-ROM

On the CD-ROM you will find:
● Printable versions of both photocopiable pages.

Name:

Imagine

■ Cut out the boxes and place them face down on the table. Take turns to pick one up, read the subject and tell the group some imaginary things about it.

■ Help each other out. You could turn your best ones into writing.

■ What would you see and hear, smell and feel? What would you find there? What does it feel like?

The contents of a Pirate's locker.	The aliens on Planet Zogg. 
The lair of the dreaded swamp monster. 	The magic forest at the other end of a rainbow. 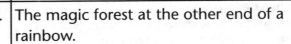
The island no one has ever visited. 	The secret tunnel under the school. 

Illustrations © 2008, Tim Archibold.

Refining punctuation in writing

They said

■ Imagine a situation in which someone said these things. What conversation could follow? Use the speech bubbles at the bottom of the page to construct a conversation.

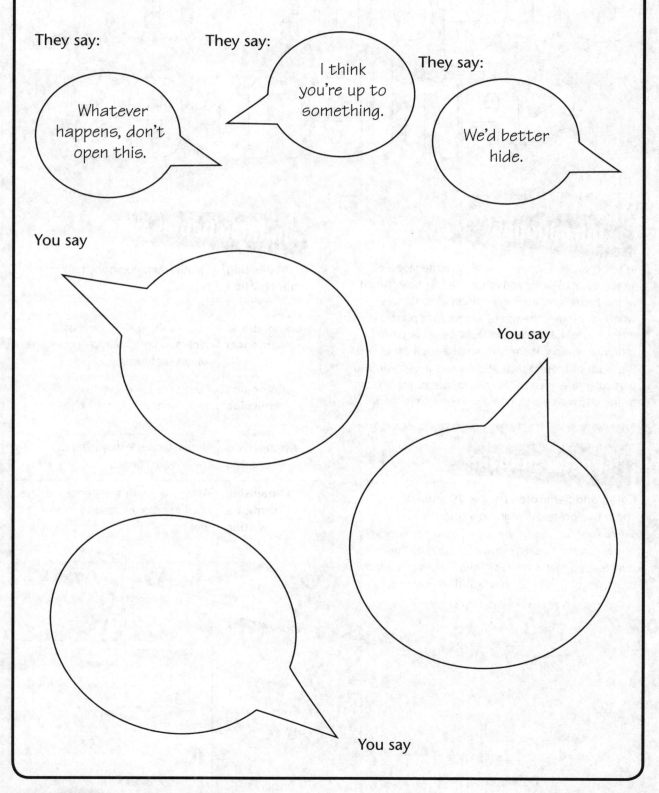

They say:

Whatever happens, don't open this.

They say:

I think you're up to something.

They say:

We'd better hide.

You say

You say

You say

Chapter 4

Organising sentences

Introduction

In this chapter, various features of sentences are either revisited or looked at for the first time. Much of the focus is on the organisation of sentences, whether through the use of appropriate punctuation or the use of particular connectives. In 'Organising sentence writing' there is an emphasis on securing the place of these punctuation marks in writing, with particular reference to the importance of the concept of the clause as a vital guide to sentence writing.

Poster notes

Colon and Semicolon (pages 79 and 80)
These two posters explain how colons and semicolons are used. One of the most effective ways of developing children's understanding of these punctuation marks is to ask them to devise their own examples of sentences in which they are used.

In this chapter

Revisiting punctuation page 81	Identify common punctuation marks.
Commas and sentences page 85	Practise the use of commas separating grammatical boundaries within sentences.
Colon and semicolon page 89	Recognise colons and semicolons and respond to them when reading.
Connectives page 93	Understand the way in which clauses are connected.
Organising sentence writing page 97	Apply the various sentence features used to organise sentences to writing.

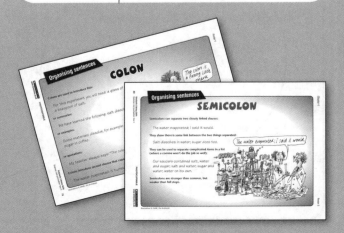

Organising sentences

COLON

Colons are used to introduce lists:

For this experiment you will need: a glass of water, a teaspoon of salt.

or summaries:

We have learned the following: salt dissolves in water....

or examples:

Some materials dissolve, for example: salt in water, sugar in coffee.

or quotations:

My teacher always says: "The colon is a funny little mark."

Colons introduce second clauses that expand or illustrate the first:

The water evaporated: it turned into water vapour.

The colon is a funny little mark

A colon separates one clause from another, without cutting the two off like a full stop.

Illustrations © 2008, Tim Archibold.

SCHOLASTIC PHOTOCOPIABLE
www.scholastic.co.uk
Scholastic Literacy Skills
Grammar and punctuation: Year 4 **79**

Organising sentences

SEMICOLON

Semicolons can separate two closely linked clauses:

The water evaporated; I said it would.

They show there is some link between the two things separated:

Salt dissolves in water; sugar does too.

They can be used to separate complicated items in a list (where a comma won't do the job so well):

Our saucers contained salt, water and sugar; salt and water; sugar and water; water on its own.

Semicolons are stronger than commas, but weaker than full stops.

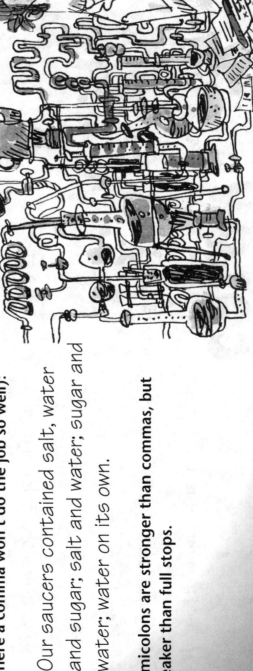

The water evaporated; I said it would.

Illustrations © 2008, Tim Archibold.

Revisiting punctuation

Objective

Identify common punctuation marks.

Background knowledge

One of the chief reasons punctuation is used is because it clarifies reading. The words in the following sentence show this at work:

Laura was sound asleep an hour after she walked into school.

When punctuated, this sentence reads:

Laura was sound asleep. An hour after, she walked into school.

Activities

The focus of these activities is on finding the places in a text where punctuation marks should be inserted. Experiencing the difficulty of reading without punctuation is followed by the children looking at different ways in which it can be used.

● **Photocopiable page 82 'Finding punctuation'**
Let the children read the unpunctuated version of this passage before reading the punctuated one. Looking at the confusions that arise and trying to make sense of the text will help them realise that without punctuation certain sections of the passage may be misread.

● **Photocopiable page 83 'Find and explain'**
Following on from the reading of 'David's omelettes', children can look for various punctuation marks in the first, punctuated version of the text. In some cases they will have looked at the rules for using a particular punctuation mark (for instance, the apostrophe). In others they will need to look closely at particular sentences in the passage to try to gauge the purpose of individual punctuation marks.

● **Photocopiable page 84 'Punctuation hunt'**
This activity encourages the children to familiarise themselves with various forms of punctuation by reading text in newspapers and magazines. Some children may need help in clarifying the task that a particular punctuation mark is performing once they have identified it in the text.

Further ideas

● **Popular punctuation marks:** Ask the children to look at different texts to see if there are any punctuation marks that appear more in some than in others. Comic stories can contain a fair quota of exclamation marks; application forms usually have many question marks.
● **Race to find:** Give the children a three-minute challenge. Explain that, working in groups of three with newspaper cuttings, they have to try to find as many punctuation marks as they can within the time limit.
● **Estimate:** Show a block of text to the children from a distance (or projected out of focus). Ask them to estimate how many full stops or speech marks they think it may contain. Having made their estimates, they can then see the text close-up or in focus to check how accurate they were.

What's on the CD-ROM

On the CD-ROM you will find:
● Printable versions of all three photocopiable pages.
● Interactive version of 'Finding punctuation'.

Name:

Finding punctuation

■ Read the two texts. What difficulties arise from the unpunctuated one?

davids omelettes

david makes brilliant omelettes davids recipe uses the following two eggs a little bit of butter grated cheese and one finely chopped mushroom it has to be chopped into really little bits and fried beforehand

first take an egg beater and beat the eggs they dont need to be very well beaten then melt the butter in a small frying pan dont let the butter get too hot pour the beaten egg mixture into the pan when it is nearly solid turn it over and sprinkle the mushrooms over it then quickly add the grated cheese and fold the omelette into a the shape of a semicircle let the cheese melt for a few moments take care the omelette doesnt overcook

david says a good omelette is not a snack my recipe its a meal in itself what do you think

David's omelettes

David makes brilliant omelettes. David's recipe uses the following: two eggs, a little bit of butter, grated cheese and one finely chopped mushroom (it has to be chopped into really little bits and fried beforehand).

First take an egg-beater and beat the eggs; they don't need to be very well beaten. Then melt the butter in a small frying pan (don't let the butter get too hot!). Pour the beaten egg mixture into the pan. When it is nearly solid, turn it over and sprinkle the mushrooms over it. Then quickly add the grated cheese and fold the omelette into the shape of a semicircle. Let the cheese melt for a few moments; take care the omelette doesn't overcook.

David says, "A good omelette is not a snack. My recipe – it's a meal in itself." What do you think?

Illustrations © 1999, Tim Archibold.

Revisiting punctuation

Find and explain

■ Read 'David's omelettes'. Look for these punctuation marks. Circle them in the passage.

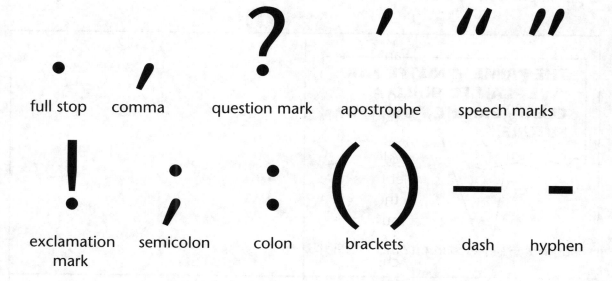

full stop   comma   question mark   apostrophe   speech marks

exclamation mark   semicolon   colon   brackets   dash   hyphen

■ In the boxes below, put a tick each time you find one of them in the text.

.	'	?	'	" "	!
full stop	comma	question mark	apostrophe	speech marks	exclamation mark

;	:	( )	—	-
semicolon	colon	brackets	dash	hyphen

■ On a separate piece of paper, explain what job each of the punctuation marks is doing.

Name:

Punctuation hunt

■ Look through a magazine and collect examples of **five** different types of punctuation. Cut out the pieces of text and paste them into the boxes. Write an explanation of what the punctuation marks are doing underneath the cuttings.

THE PRIME MINISTER SAID: "WE PLAN TO BUILD A CLEAR, BRIGHT, POSITIVE FUTURE."

comma – separating items in a list

Commas and sentences

Objective

Practise the use of commas, separating grammatical boundaries within sentences.

Background knowledge

A sentence can consist of one or more clauses. A clause is a group of words linked to a particular verb. It can include a verb and a subject and look like a sentence in itself. So in the sentence *I like coffee, you like tea* there are two clauses. 'I' is the subject of the verb 'like' in one of the clauses; 'you and 'like' make up the subject and verb of the other. Commas can mark the boundaries between clauses. This can be seen in the 'coffee' and 'tea' sentence.

Commas can also demarcate relative clauses. These are clauses that slot into a sentence, giving extra information about things already mentioned. A sentence could state *Mr Carter mended our cooker*. A clause could be inserted to clarify that Mr Carter lives next door. This is additional information to develop meaning and the sentence would function without it. The inserted clause is marked off by commas: *Mr Carter, who lives next door, mended our cooker.*

Activities

As children develop more complex sentence structures in their writing they can use commas to demarcate clauses. Once they can see the potential for a space in between two commas (or before or after a single comma) into which they can place information, they will find the structure of a sentence easier to understand and a more complex sentence easier to write.

● **Photocopiable page 86 'Slot into a sentence'**

Ask the children to look at each sentence and see if they can spot where the extra information provided in the clause can be placed. It is important that they read their new sentences as they construct them to check that they make sense.

● **Photocopiable page 87 'Clauses'**

Ask the children to look at each sentence to make sure that one of the commas is in the right place. They can then say the sentences out loud, reading only the comma they've selected, to help them to decide which commas to remove.

● **Photocopiable page 88 'Dead worried'**

Arrange the children into groups of four to six. Ask them to work in pairs, using a coloured pencil to insert the commas into the passage. They can then compare their completed sheets with another pair's (copying their commas onto the other pair's sheet using a different colour). Encourage them to discuss any differences of opinion. Round off the activity by telling the children where the commas are placed in the original text:

Further ideas

● **Taking sentences apart:** Provide the children with other texts which they can look at closely to see where commas have been used to demarcate grammatical boundaries. When they have identified the separate parts of a sentence, they should focus on the question: *What distinctive thing does each part say?*

● **Rewriting sentences:** Reviewing some recent pieces of their writing, the children can look at some of the sentences they have used to see if they could have given more information. Could they have put in a relative clause to identify or explain something more clearly?

What's on the CD-ROM

On the CD-ROM you will find:
● Printable versions of all three photocopiable pages.
● Answers to 'Slot into a sentence' and 'Clauses'.
● Interactive version of 'Clauses'.

start in
class - tried as
per.

Commas and sentences

Slot into a sentence

■ Each of these sentences has a slip of information between two commas. The slip can be inserted somewhere in the sentence.

■ Cut out the sentence strip and the slip. For example:

| The big bull escaped and ran through the village. | , the fiercest on the farm, |

■ Mark the sentence at the point where you think the slip belongs.
Read the whole sentence. For example:

| The big bull | , the fiercest on the farm, | escaped and ran through the village. |

■ Does it read well? Does it sound right?

■ Cut the sentence strip in two at the right point, place the slip in the space in between and stick the new longer sentence onto a sheet of paper.

■ Now do the same with these sentences and slips.

Laura starts Nursery today.	, my sister,
My friend is a great swimmer.	, called Sam Watson,
My brother dressed smartly today.	, who is usually a scruff,
For my birthday I want a party.	, in March,
Our poplar tree blew over in the storm.	, the one on the school field,
Ms Shell repaired our light switch.	, our school caretaker,
I might join the school chess team.	, if I get a chance,
When she gets home my mum has a sleep.	, worn out and tired,

Commas and sentences

Clauses

He reached out a hand catching the ball.
As it was raining playtime was abandoned.
There is football practice on Tuesday I think.

These can sound odd when you read them.

In each of these sentences one thing is said and then another. There are two chunks. Each of the chunks contains a verb. These chunks are called clauses. A comma separates one clause from another clause.

He reached out a hand, catching the ball.
As it was raining, playtime was abandoned.
There is football practice on Tuesday, I think.

Readers are supposed to pause at the comma.

■ Look at these sentences. Each contains three commas but only needs **one**.
■ Rewrite the sentences, leaving out two of the commas. Remember to check your sentence by reading it aloud.

She, swung the bat, hitting, the ball.

_____

You want, your coat, I, suppose.

_____

Nassim, walked, slowly, missing the bus.

_____

The plug came out, of the computer, losing, all our work.

_____

The dog, barked, making, the cat jump.

_____

Illustrations © 1999, Tim Archibold.

Name:

Dead worried

■ Replace **thirteen** missing commas (remember the title!).

Calm down Mr King

Mr King is my school teacher. He's OK even if he gets a bit worked up some days.

Today is one of those days. Behind his steaming glasses his eyes are glazed with

emotion.

"So Year 6 if we are going to produce some good creative writing for you to

take home to your suffering parents we've got to have creative input. Do you

know what input means Corky?"

Corky my best mate blinks and says "Input. Like output but different. Yes. Sure.

Input. Let me think. Um. Putting something in. Yeah."

Mr King glares at him. "That was a lucky guess Corky." He removes his glasses

wipes them blots the damp patch on his forehead and breathes heavily.

from *Dead Worried* by Moya Simons

Colon and semicolon

Objective

Recognise colons and semicolons and respond to them when reading.

Background knowledge

- **Colons are used to:**
  - introduce lists: *For this experiment you will need: a glass of water, a teaspoon of salt.*
  - summaries: *We have learned the following: salt dissolves in water…*
  - examples: *Some materials dissolve, for example: salt in water, sugar in coffee.*
  - quotations: *My teacher always says: 'The colon is a funny little mark.'*
  - introduce second clauses that expand or illustrate the first: *The water evaporated: it turned into water vapour.*
  - separates one clause from another: without cutting the two off like a full stop.
- **Semicolons can:**
  - separate two closely linked clauses: *The water evaporated; I said it would.*
  - show there is some link between the two things separated: *Salt dissolves in water; sugar does too.*
  - can be used to separate complicated items in a list (where a comma won't do the job so well): *Our saucers contained salt, water and sugar; salt and water; sugar and water; water on its own.*
  - Semicolons are stronger than commas, but weaker than full stops.

Activities

Both of these punctuation marks are classic examples of that great rule of punctuation: if in doubt, leave it out. However, when looking at some of the examples above, it is clear they serve a useful purpose.

- **Photocopiable page 90 'Colon and semicolon'**
The text on this sheet, explaining the ways that colons and semicolons can be used, links to the examples on photocopiable page 91. This sheet can also be used as a frame for the children to devise their own examples for the various uses of the two punctuation marks.
- **Photocopiable page 91 'Examples – colons and semicolons'**
Having read photocopiable page 90, invite the children to find one example of each type. Encourage them to use the examples on the sheet as a model for trying to produce their own sample sentences containing colons and semicolons. Ask them to choose three sentences and explain why they used colons or semicolons.
- **Photocopiable page 92 'Colon or semicolon?'**
The children insert the punctuation mark they believe to be appropriate, using the examples in the previous activity as a guide. The examples are closely modelled on each other so, having completed this activity, it would be a good idea to ask them to look through some of the books in the classroom to find other, more varied uses of the colon and semicolon.

Further ideas

- **Writing type:** Both these punctuation marks perform a particular role in certain types of writing. For example, they can clarify the explanation of a science task or the listing of items used in a technology project. As these punctuation marks are introduced to the children, look at texts across the curriculum, focusing on writing in which their use could be reinforced.
- **Quotes book:** Ask the children to include colons when recording quotations in a 'quotes book'. They can staple some pages of A5 paper together and, over time, record the words members of their family or people in their neighbourhood are renowned for saying.

What's on the CD-ROM

On the CD-ROM you will find:
- Printable versions of all three photocopiable pages.
- Answers to 'Colon and semicolon' / 'Examples – colons and semicolons' and 'Colon or semicolon?'.
- Interactive versions of 'Colon and semicolon' 'Examples – colons and semicolons'.

Name:

Colon and semicolon

Colon and semicolon

■ Meet two new types of punctuation.

Colon :
Used to introduce a list

```
[                                                    ]
```

or a summary

```
[                                                    ]
```

or an example

```
[                                                    ]
```

or a quotation.

```
[                                                    ]
```

Introduces a second clause that explains the first.

```
[                                                    ]
```

Semicolon ;
Used to separate two closely linked clauses.

```
[                                                    ]
```

Shows there is some link between the two things it separates.

```
[                                                    ]
```

Can be used to separate complicated items in a list (where a comma won't do the job so well).

```
[                                                    ]
```

Colon and semicolon

Examples – colons and semicolons

■ Cut out the examples and match them to the explanations.

My teacher always says: "The colon is a funny little mark."
We have learned the following: salt dissolves in water…
The water evaporated; I said it would.
Salt dissolves in water; sugar does too.
Our saucers contained salt, water and sugar; salt and water; sugar and water; water on its own.
The water evaporated: it turned into water vapour.
For this experiment you will need: a glass of water, a teaspoon of salt.
Some materials dissolve, for example: salt in water, sugar in coffee.

For this experiment you will need: a glass of water, a teaspoon of salt, three tadpoles and a small child

tadpoles

small child

Illustrations © 1999, Tim Archibold.

Name:

Colon and semicolon

Colon or semicolon?

■ Look at these twelve sentences. In each there is a space. Should it have a colon or a semicolon?

1 There are some things that annoy me ⬚ my little brother, my teacher, nasty dogs.

2 I like playtime ⬚ Josh does too.

3 My grandad always says ⬚ "Mind your manners, young lad."

4 This story teaches us the lesson ⬚ don't count your chickens before they're hatched.

5 My pet snail packed his shell, said goodbye and slithered away ⬚ he left!

6 Playtime was cancelled ⬚ we were not pleased!

7 It was raining at playtime ⬚ yesterday was the same.

8 Here is what you need ⬚ an egg, a candle, a piece of string.

■ Pick two of your sentences and explain why you chose the mark you used.

Sentence number _____	Sentence number _____
I used a _____	I used a _____
because _____	because _____
_____	_____
_____	_____

Connectives

Understand the way in which clauses are connected.

Background knowledge

Clauses are units of language including at least a subject and (usually) a verb. They can be parts of sentences or whole sentences. The space between clauses can be marked by connecting words or punctuation. For example, two clauses can be separated by a comma: *I went to school, I think.*

Or a semicolon: *I went to school; that was my first mistake.*

There are also connective words that can link clauses. These words include conjunctions such as 'and', and 'but' and connecting adverbs such as 'also' and 'therefore'. For example: *I went to school and I regretted it* or *I went to school, but I got out at home time.*

There are four ways in which clauses can be connected. These are:
- **Addition:** words to add, such as 'and' and 'also'.
- **Opposition:** words to oppose, such as 'but' and 'however'.
- **Cause:** things causing other things – words such as 'because', 'so' and 'therefore'.
- **Time:** the times when things happened – words such as 'then' and 'after'.

Activities

Variety is the spice of connection in language. An important aim is to develop children's awareness of a range of ways of connecting clauses and escape the endless uses of the word 'and' encountered in so many stories. With this in mind, the activities should be accompanied by children reviewing their own uses of connecting devices in their writing.

- **Photocopiable page 94 'Connect'**
The sentences can be completed using the connectives given on the sheet. Some connectives will need to be used more than once, but encourage the children to choose as wide a variety as possible.
- **Photocopiable page 95 'Connective jobs'**
This activity, in which the children identify different types of connective and explain their usage, can be supplemented by the use of real leaflets from shops, libraries and so on.
- **Photocopiable page 96 'Clause shading'**
In this activity children look at the clause style of a classic author. As a class, compare E Nesbitt's writing with the style of some modern-day writers.

Further ideas

- **Counting types:** Provide the children with different types of texts and ask them to look through them carefully to see if certain connectives feature more in some texts than in others – for example, they may find explanatory texts have more causal connections and narratives more temporal ones.
- **And:** Focus on the use of the word 'and' – ask the children to look through their own uses of 'and' in their story writing. Could they have used a better alternative?

What's on the CD-ROM

On the CD-ROM you will find:
- Printable versions of all three photocopiable pages.
- Answers to 'Connect' and 'Connective jobs'.
- Interactive version of 'Connect'.

Name:

Connectives

Connect

Words can be used to connect two bits of a sentence together. Bits of a sentence that say something are called clauses.

■ Look at these broken sentences and find a connecting word you think fits between the two clauses. You could use the same word twice, if you need to.

Connecting words		
and	also	but
because	so	therefore
then	and then	after

We can't go out _____ it is raining.

Playtime was starting _____ we lined up.

We were all ready to go _____ a message came saying it was raining.

Our teacher said, "It is raining outside _____ it's indoor play."

I really wanted to go out _____ we had to stay in.

Playtime is fun, _____ playtime is healthy.

Staying in is miserable _____ we are allowed to read comics.

I read a funny comic _____ I read a football comic.

We played one game _____ playtime ended.

Our teacher came back _____ lessons started.

The rain has stopped _____ we can't go out.

We will go out _____ we have had our dinners.

PHOTOCOPIABLE

SCHOLASTIC
www.scholastic.co.uk

Connectives

Connective jobs

Clauses can be connected in different ways.

Some connecting words add clauses together:
I like chips **and** I like them from the chip shop.

Some connecting words oppose one clause against another:
I like chips **but** I can't afford them.

Some connecting words show how one thing caused another:
I ate some chips **because** I was hungry.
or was caused by another:
I was hungry **so** I bought some chips.

Some connecting words show the times when things happened:
I had some chips, **then** I went and had some more.

■ Look at the connecting words in this leaflet. Highlight them and note the job they are doing.

The Space ♥
the heart of the city

Outside, city life bustles on but inside the Space you can take a break. Attractions include:

Gallery: The central exhibition area currently houses touring art exhibitions and work by local artists. Works by Space artists are displayed then sold at our monthly art sale.

Artspace: A space where artists hold workshops. Children's art classes are run on Saturday morning, also during half-term holidays.

Café: After touring the exhibitions you can relax on the terrace café. Enjoy one of our range of cakes and drinks and then have another trip round the exhibition!

Drama classes: These will start next spring but are not running at present because of a lack of funding.

After-school classes: In the coming term we will be starting after school art classes so we are currently offering places. Please ask at the front desk.

There is no charge for admission but we do encourage visitors to make a voluntary contribution of £1 so we can meet our running costs.

Name:

Connectives

Clause shading

Clauses can be connected or separated by:
- connecting words
- commas
- full stops.

■ Look at this extract from a story written over a hundred years ago. Read the sentences and find the separate clauses and the way they are connected or separated.

> Remember, a clause is like a mini-sentence with its own verb.

Chapter 2
I am afraid the last chapter was rather dull. It is always dull in books when people talk and talk and don't do anything, but I was obliged to put it in, or else you wouldn't have understood all the rest. The best part of books is when things are happening. That is the best part of real things too. That is why I shall not tell you in this story about the days when nothing happened. You will not catch me saying, 'thus the sad days passed slowly by' – or 'the years rolled on their weary course' – or 'time went on' – because it is silly; of course time goes on – whether you say so or not. So I shall just tell you the nice, interesting parts – and in between you will understand that we had our meals and got up and and went to bed, and dull things like that.

from The Treasure Seekers by E Nesbitt

Illustrations © 1999, Tim Archibold.

Organising sentence writing

Objective

Apply the various sentence features used to organise sentences to writing.

Writing focus

Having looked at a range of features that organise sentences, this section gathers together ways in which children can turn their work on punctuation and connection into a focus on writing.

Skills to writing

● Punctuation in context

Having ascertained the use of the range of punctuation marks covered in an activity such as that on photocopiable pages 82 and 83, children now need to take these examples and apply them to a range of texts. It's not enough just to find the mark – children should also be encouraged to explain the usage. If, for example, a colon is used, they need to see whether it starts a list or introduces speech. One useful resource is Martin Waddell's picture book *Owl Babies* (Walker Books) – apart from being a great story it's also awash with punctuation!

● Checklist

The children should start to maintain their own punctuation checklist, checking off their own deployment of the range of marks in their writing. This should be handled with a sense of progression, with the sentence ending marks – full stop, question mark and exclamation mark – tackled first. Then, within sentences, children should target the use of speech marks. Parallel with this they should look to use commas in lists. The other marks follow on after these.

● Clauses! Clauses! Clauses!

Clauses are vital. The children need to understand what a clause is, to identify clauses in reading and be mindful of them in writing. Clauses are the main way in which children can extend their own sentence writing. Understand the nature of a clause and you can connect them using connectives and separate them with commas. Children need to know the importance of this aspect of sentence grammar – it's about clauses.

● Persuasive connections

Look out for the connections that are made in persuasive texts. It's here that a point is made and a 'therefore' or a 'so' moves to extend the case being made. In their own writing of persuasive texts children should be encouraged to use appropriate connectives. They should aim to structure their case such that a 'because' argues back to evidence or a 'therefore' hammers home the thrust of their case.

● Connectives in varied texts

Look out for the jobs being done by connectives in a range of texts and encourage children to take the sentences they find as models for their own writing.

Activities

● Photocopiable page 99 'The Elves and the Shoemaker'

This text contains a number of colons and semicolons – more than writers would use today. Ask the children to read the story in groups, looking closely at how the colons and semicolons are being used. Where would they not have used them if the text had been written by them today? Help them understand the functions that the punctuation marks (colons and semicolons) are performing in each context. The children should consider the way these marks prompt them to pause – how different are they from full stops?

It is interesting to see how colons and semicolons have 'separated out' from each other in their usage in modern writing, having much more clearly defined functions. In 'The Elves and the Shoemaker' many of the colons would be substituted for a dash today (for example: *At last he had nothing left in the world but a small piece of leather – just enough to make one final pair of shoes* or *As for the shoemaker – he lived well the rest of his life*). Other colons would be replaced by full stops, especially in writing for young children (*We must do something for them. We shall make them some clothes and boots to keep them warm*), or semicolons (*Each night the shoemaker cut out his shoes; each morning he returned to find them expertly finished*).

● Photocopiable page 100 'Connectives'

This photocopiable sheet presents the four different types of connective that children can use in their writing.

It can be used as a way of encouraging children to think of new and varied ways of constructing sentences in their writing. It can also be used as a way of challenging them to revisit their writing to find what sort of connectives they have used.

One activity that can be done is to ask children to think of various sentences on a particular subject, trying to use the different types of connective. The varied types of connection used can act as a stimulus for thinking.

Write on

● Sentence expansion

Ask the children to write simple sentences on strips of paper and then look to see where an extra clause could be inserted between commas, or whether an addition could be made using a semicolon. As they do this they can cut up the sentence, add a strip in one place, insert one in another. Make sure that they stick down and display their modified versions as they provide an effective reminder of how writers can rejig sentences.

● Protest

Ask the children to think of something they would like to change. For example, would they like a longer playtime? Then they need to campaign for it. Encourage them to come up with a cause on which they could mount a campaign and for which they could produce a leaflet or poster, using the connectives they have learned to push home their argument.

● Clause partners

No, it's not Santa's new firm of solicitors but children working in pairs to develop clauses. Two children writing sentences together can be an effective way of pushing for more extended, complex sentences. As they engage in their writing they each need to become a clause in a sentence. If the text is a persuasive piece and one of them is suggesting they should write 'Fruit is good for you', the second person needs to suggest how they could insert a clause in the sentence (for example, 'because it is full of the things you need'). Somehow, two people sharing this task can make it plainer, as each of them physically becomes part of the sentence.

What's on the CD-ROM

On the CD-ROM you will find:
● Printable versions of both photocopiable pages.

Organising sentence writing

The Elves and the Shoemaker

■ The use of punctuation changes over time. Sometimes older texts, like this one by the Brothers Grimm, contain more punctuation marks than modern texts. Read the story, find the colons and semicolons and look at how they are being used.

There was once an honest shoemaker who worked very hard; but no matter how much he worked, he never earned enough to live. At last he had nothing left in the world but a small piece of leather: just enough to make one final pair of shoes. The shoemaker cut the shoes out carefully and laid them out on his bench; they would be ready for when he returned in the morning. That night he said his prayers as usual and slept peacefully.

What a surprise greeted him next day: there on the workbench, was the most beautiful pair of shoes the shoemaker had ever seen! Every stitch was perfect; the craftsmanship was faultless. Later that day a gentleman came into the shop and asked to try the shoes. Imagine: they fitted him perfectly and he was so pleased that he payed handsomely for them. Now the shoemaker could buy more leather.

And so the days continued. Each night the shoemaker cut out his shoes: each morning he returned to find them expertly finished. He began to grow prosperous again.

One evening around Christmas time, the shoemaker made a decision: 'I want to stay up tonight,' he said to his wife, 'to see just who is making my shoes for me.' So they hid themselves in the workroom and waited.

At the stroke of midnight they heard the sound of tiny feet scuttling across the floor: two, tiny, naked men scrambled up to the shoemaker's bench, where they sat and began to sew and stitch the pieces of leather; working so swiftly that in no time at all they had finished the shoes. Then the two little men disappeared as quickly as they had come.

The shoemaker and his wife were astonished: they had never imagined that elves had been helping them. 'Those two little men have made us wealthy, husband,' said the wife. 'We must do something for them: we shall make them some clothes and boots to keep them warm.'

When the little men came that night, they fell on the clothing with delight; they quickly dressed themselves and danced and capered about the workroom – and right out of the door, never to be seen again.

As for the shoemaker: he lived well the rest of his life.

retold by Jackie Andrews

Text © 2008, Jackie Andrews; Illustrations © 1999, Tim Archibold.

■SCHOLASTIC
www.scholastic.co.uk   **PHOTOCOPIABLE**   Scholastic Literacy Skills
Grammar and punctuation: Year 4   **99**

Name:

Organising sentence writing

Connectives

■ Look at the different types of connectives. Can you use these in your writing? Add to the examples with sentences you have used.

Type of connection	Addition	Opposition	Cause	Time
Function	words to add things	words to oppose things	things causing other things	the times when things happened
Examples	*and* *also*	*but* *however*	*because* *so* *therefore*	*then* *and then* *after*
	I like my school and I like my classroom.	I went out to play but I felt ill.	The match was called off because it was raining.	I went to the shop then I called for my friend.

Illustrations © 1999, Tim Archibold.

Chapter 5

Changing words

Introduction

This chapter looks at various types of word ending, including comparative endings and pluralisation. Once again we are encountering features of grammar that are more than just spelling rules. They provide ways of looking at how certain word types, such as nouns and verbs, operate. Much of this chapter involves changing one type of word to another and looking at how this affects the form of the word.

Poster notes

Verb masher (page 102)
This is a large version of the chart used in 'Verb endings'. It provides an opportunity for the class to suggest and use their own examples in the chart.

Plurals (page 103)
The 'Plurals' poster shows the various ways words are altered to change a singular noun into a plural.

In this chapter

Verb endings page 104	Learn the ways in which verbs and verb endings can change.
Comparative endings page 108	Understand the ways in which comparative endings change.
Pluralisation page 112	Understand the ways in which noun endings change for plurals.
Changes and word class page 116	Use changes that can be made in words to identify word class.
Choose the 'write' words page 120	Apply, and develop the use of, rules for the changing of words in writing.

Changing words

Verb masher

Base form	-s form	-ing participle	-ed past form

Illustrations © 2008, Tim Archibold.

Changing words

Plurals

Usual rule

The usual way of turning a singular noun to a plural is to add an **s**.
For example:

cat → *cats*　　　*spoon* → *spoons*

But if the singular ends in any of the following ways, then the plural is sometimes made in a different way.

Singular endings	Usual rule	Example	
y after a consonant	Remove **y**, add **ies**	*fairy*	→ *fairies*
y after a vowel	add **s**	*day*	→ *days*
o after a consonant	add **es**	*potato*	→ *potatoes*
o after a vowel	add **s**	*video*	→ *videos*
with a sound like **s**, such as **ss**, **sh**, **tch**, **x**, **z**	add **es**	*kiss* *wish*	→ *kisses* → *wishes*
with a **ch** sound like **ch**, **tch**	add **es**	*perch* *watch*	→ *perches* → *watches*
f	Remove **f**, add **ves***	*thief*	→ *thieves*

* For some words nowadays, it is acceptable to retain the **f** and just add **s** (for example, **roofs**).

Illustrations © 2008, Tim Archibold.

Verb endings

Objective

Learn the ways in which verbs and verb endings can change.

Background knowledge

There are four common forms of verbs.

- **The plain form:** *cook*.
- **The '-s' form used, at times, for the third-person singular:** *he cooks, she cooks*.
- **The '-ing' participle indicating that the action is ongoing:** *I was cooking, I am cooking, I will be cooking*.
- **The past tense '-ed' form:** *I cooked*.

    A number of verbs take these regular endings. However, there are some that don't. Interestingly enough they tend to be very important ones such as 'I am', 'I can', 'I do'.

Activities

Children need an understanding of the common forms verbs can take, coupled with an awareness that exceptions are rife. These activities present the exceptions as well as the rules.

- **Photocopiable page 105 'Verb masher'**
This activity takes the children through the various endings that regular verbs can take. Remind them that if they find it difficult to work out what ending a verb should have, it is helpful to think of an example of its use. It is easier to think of the third-person use of the word 'cook', for example, if you think of a context in which you would say the word, such as in the sentence *He cooks in the kitchen*.

- **Photocopiable page 106 'Shaun's story'**
Various forms of verbs used in this story have been removed, leaving only the base form. The children have to write in the correct forms. Remind them to use the context to figure out how the base form should be altered. There are a number of irregular verbs in the story, so they will need to rely less on the rules, saying the sentences aloud to hear if they make sense.

- **Photocopiable page 107 'Make the change'**
The children are asked to fill in the tables in this activity to change the base form of the verb to the third person and to the past tense. Looking at the context of each sentence will help the children to provide the correct verb ending. This activity can be used as a starting point for looking at which verbs follow a rule and which do not.

Further ideas

- **Sorting verbs:** Compile a large chart of verbs, asking the children to add more verbs as they encounter them. Divide the chart into two sections according to whether the verb takes on regular forms or irregular.
- **Dictionary forms:** Ask the children to look through dictionaries to find verbs that follow a regular form. In many dictionaries the other forms of a verb are listed along with the base form.

 **What's on the CD-ROM**

On the CD-ROM you will find:
- Printable versions of all three photocopiable pages.
- Answers to all three photocopiable pages.
- Interactive versions of 'Verb masher' and 'Shaun's story'.

Verb endings

Verb masher

One verb can appear in lots of different forms:

I kick

He kicks

I am kicking

I kicked

■ Look at the verbs in the tray and write them out in the correct form in the verb masher. Look at some of the changes that happen. Are there times when changes you expect don't happen?

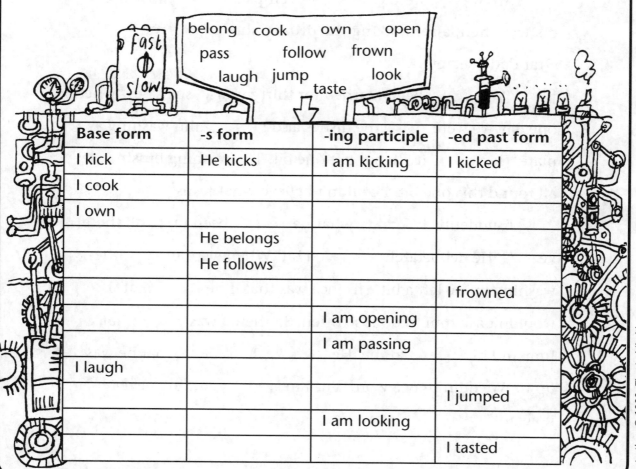

Base form	-s form	-ing participle	-ed past form
I kick	He kicks	I am kicking	I kicked
I cook			
I own			
	He belongs		
	He follows		
			I frowned
		I am opening	
		I am passing	
I laugh			
			I jumped
		I am looking	
			I tasted

Illustrations © 1999, Tim Archibold.

Name:

Verb endings

Shaun's story

■ Look at this story. It contains verbs printed in the simple form. They need to be changed. Write the correct version over each verb (printed in italic), making sure that it fits in with the story.

Take care! Lots of these verbs change in different ways from the usual.

Yesterday I *go* to my grans. I go there every Wednesday after school. She *make* my tea and then we do the dishes. She *say* I do them much better than my grandad. We always make a cup of tea. I have orange juice and she *have* tea with one sugar. While we're *have* our drink she *tell* me a story.

Anyway, yesterday I *have* chips and we *do* the dishes. Then, after making the drinks, she *tell* me Grandad's secret.

"We *have* been married for thirty years," she said, "when one day we were *do* the dishes and I *see* him washing a plate. He *wash* it all, but left one bit. The washing brush *go* all round this one bit. I couldn't believe what I was *see* !"

"Suddenly, I *know* what he *have* been up to all these years." "He deliberately *leave* a bit! Whenever he *do* the washing up he left a bit. His idea was that if he *do* that, I wouldn't ask him to do it so often. So there I was, *stare* at him and he *look* at me. He *know* I *know* what he was up to. We didn't say a word. But I'm you... he never *do* it again!"

Verb endings

Make the change

■ Fill in the spaces in each table.

■ Change the verbs to the third person.

Every day I make my sandwiches.	Every day he _____ his sandwiches.
I only laugh at jokes if they are funny.	My brother only _____ at jokes if they are funny.
I have to do my homework now.	She _____ to do her homework now.
At the weekend I do some cleaning.	At the weekend he _____ some cleaning.
On Fridays I go to science club.	On Fridays she _____ to science club.
If I lose something I usually find it behind my bed.	If he _____ something he usually _____ it behind his bed.
I like to read comics.	He _____ to read comics.
I am brilliant!	She _____ brilliant!

■ Change the verbs to the past tense.

Every day I make my sandwiches.	Yesterday I _____ my sandwiches.
I laugh at the jokes because they are funny.	I _____ at the jokes because they were funny.
At the weekend I do some cleaning.	Last weekend I _____ some cleaning.
When I lose a sock I look for it.	When I _____ a sock I looked for it.
On Fridays I go to science club.	Last Friday I _____ to science club.
I like the clowns.	When we went to the circus I _____ the clowns.
I have to do my homework now.	Earlier on, I _____ to do my homework.
Today, school is brilliant!	Yesterday, school _____ brilliant!

■ What do you notice about the changes to the verbs?

Comparative endings

Objective

Understand the ways in which comparative endings change.

Background knowledge

Comparative and superlative forms of adjectives are usually made by adding 'er' and 'est' to the plain (or nominative) adjective, for example *sharp → sharper*. If the adjective ends in 'y' the 'y' is changed to 'i' before the addition is made, for example *happy → happier*.

If the adjective consists of one syllable and there is only one vowel before the final consonant, then the final consonant is doubled before the ending is added, for example *sad → sadder*.

Activities

The initial activity looks at changes to adjective endings. These are then tried out within the contexts of reading and writing poetry and a critical reading of advertising.

● **Photocopiable page 109 'Comparatives and superlatives'**
The notes about adjective endings in 'Background knowledge' (see above) are important here. The children can use this activity as a way of applying the rules as well as figuring out which words are exceptions. Conclude the activity by asking the children to check their answers with others in their group. Often other children will notice missed rules or odd results.

● **Photocopiable page 110 'Liars'**
Children can use shared reading to read the poem with their group, or the poem can be read in pairs. They could even act it out. Eventually the poem can be used as a model for writing their own 'liars' poem. They can use the same build-up of nominative, comparative and superlative but find their own adjectives. As with the original, they can take an idea and build around it using appropriate text.

● **Photocopiable page 111 'Advert words'**
Advert jingles such as 'Only the crumbliest, flakiest chocolate' make use of various forms of adjectives. Seek out examples of different adjectives used in adverts for the class to analyse, letting the children watch the adverts on television (copyright permitting). Alternatively they can do the collecting task at home, finding examples in their evening viewing.

Further ideas

● **Adjective advertising:** Ask the children to devise a slogan or jingle for a new product. They can draw upon their understanding of various adjective forms when they are producing their own example.
● **List the exceptions:** The children can build up a list of adjectives to which the two rules apply – that is, those ending in 'y' and those where the final consonant needs to be doubled.

What's on the CD-ROM

On the CD-ROM you will find:
● Printable versions of all three photocopiable pages.
● Answers to 'Comparatives and superlatives'.
● Interactive version of 'Comparatives and superlatives'.

Comparative endings

Comparatives and superlatives

Adjectives can take three forms. There is the plain adjective, sometimes called the **nominative**; the adjective that compares, the **comparative**; and the adjective that beats them all, the **superlative**.

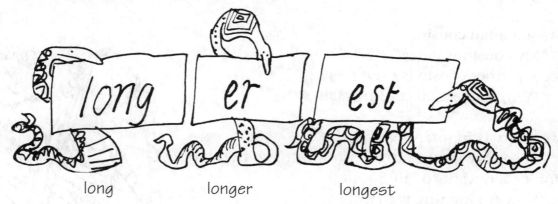

long   longer   longest

■ Look at the adjectives in the table below and fill in the missing spaces.

But remember, some could be irregular:

good   →   better   →   best

and some longer adjectives may take the other forms using **more** and **most**.

beautiful   →   more beautiful   →   most beautiful

Nominative	Comparative	Superlative
tall		
silly		
careful		
	shorter	
sad		
		happiest
		quietest
	more different	
cold		
	cooler	
	hotter	
		oldest
high		
	smaller	
		lowest

Illustrations © 1999, Tim Archibold.

Name:

Comparative endings

Liars

- Read the poem out loud in your group. You could each take one of the parts.
- Look for comparative and superlative adjectives. The poem contains some strange examples.

"I've got a tall cousin."
   "My cousin is taller."
"So! My other cousin is even taller."
   "Well, my second cousin is tallest!"

"My aunty is frightening."
   "My aunty is more frightening. She's so frightening
I don't even want to talk about it."
   "How frightening is that?"
   "Most frightening!"

"My bedroom is terrible."
   "My bedroom is terribler."
"My bedroom is terriblest."
   "Oh… right… Mine's just the most terrible."

"My gran is potty."
   "My gran is pottier."
"My gran is pottiest."
   "My gran potties the pottiest."

"My best friend is slimy."
   "My best friend is slimier."
"My friend's friend is the slimiest."
   "I know someone slimier than that."
"I'm not so sure. He is so slimy he can't walk without slipping!"
   "So! My second-best friend's so slimy he doesn't walk – he slithers!"
"I don't care – you're still my best friend."
   "How sweet."

"I'm a big liar."
   "I'm a bigger liar."
"I don't believe you."
   "Nor do I!"

- Now try to write your own poem using adjectives in the same way.

Illustrations © 1999, Tim Archibold.

Scholastic Literacy Skills
Grammar and punctuation: Year 4

PHOTOCOPIABLE

SCHOLASTIC
www.scholastic.co.uk

Comparative endings

Advert words

■ Find adverts in a newspaper or magazine. Watch a few on the television. Look for them on billboards.

■ Look for nominative, comparative and superlative adjectives. Write some of the strings of words in the spaces below.

Nominative	Comparative	Superlative

Pluralisation

Objective

Understand the ways in which noun endings change for plurals.

Background knowledge

The general idea of 'adding an "s" to make a plural' is subject to a number of exceptions. In many of the rules shown in the table below there are alterations that occur when the 's' is added. In addition to these, there are other pluralisations that are irregular (for example, 'child' and 'children'). Other examples of exceptions include words such as 'sheep' and 'trousers', which do not change at all in the plural form.

Activities

The regularity of these rules is on the teacher's side when it comes to teaching pluralisation. They provide clear help to children in forming plurals. The list provided on poster page 103 'Plurals' is an invaluable guide to the pluralisation of nouns.

● **Photocopiable page 113 'Add an 's'?'**
Part of the skill employed by language users is the instinctive feel for what is correct. We are so immersed in its use we instinctively react to spellings or word forms that just don't sound right. This is a skill children will use as they try pluralising the words given on the photocopiable sheet. One approach to the activity is to go through the input section of the machine on the sheet as a class, putting an 's' at the end of each of the words. This will probably elicit the immediate reaction from the children that *It doesn't look right* or *We don't say 'childs'!*

● **Photocopiable page 114 'Make the plural'**
As for the previous photocopiable, the children need to rely on what they feel is correct in an instinctive way when they choose the plural form of each word. In this activity, by eliminating the words that they know are wrong, the children may find it easier to decide on which word is correct.

● **Photocopiable page 115 'Random nouns'**
In this activity the children are asked to find nouns – any texts can be used – and change them from singular to plural or vice versa. Remind them to refer to the rules for plural endings (see poster page 103), and to be aware that they are likely to encounter the pluralisation of words that are exceptions to the rules.

Further ideas

● **Explain the error:** Children can take the rules chart on poster page 103 'Plurals' and use it as a way of reviewing their own spelling. If they have some writing they did in a previous year stored in a record folder, ask them to read through their work carefully to see where they missed out on certain rules.

● **New plurals:** Looking at contemporary comics or pop and computer magazines, children can find new nouns, such as terms in computer jargon (for example, 'byte') or words that are creeping into general speech (for example, 'geek'), and form their plurals.

What's on the CD-ROM

On the CD-ROM you will find:
● Printable versions of all three photocopiable pages.
● Answers to 'Add an 's'?' and 'Make the plural'.
● Interactive version of 'Add an 's'?'.

Pluralisation

Add an 's'?

The rule we often use to make a plural is 'add an **s**'.

■ Look at the nouns in the plural sorter. Sort the ones that follow the 'add **s**' rule from the ones that don't. Write down the plural words in the correct section of the machine.

box   man   child   tree   bus   tooth
van   wish   leaf
sister   sheep   foot   path   boot
trousers   fence   fish
wolf   woman
glass   shop   knife   plate

'add **s**'   'another rule'

Illustrations © 1999, Tim Archibold.

Name:

Pluralisation

Make the plural

■ Read the poster for making plurals.

■ Look at these singular nouns. Each is followed by three possible plurals. Circle the correct plural for each noun.

cat	(cates	catts	cats)
baby	(babys	babies	babeys)
boy	(boies	boyes	boys)
diary	(diaries	diares	diarys)
dish	(dishs	disheys	dishes)
fox	(foxeys	foxs	foxes)
garden	(garda	gardens	gardeens)
guess	(guesss	guessies	guesses)
hutch	(hutchs	hutches	hutchos)
lady	(ladies	ladeys	lads)
match	(matches	matchoes	matchs)
piano	(pianos	pianoes	pianoos)
place	(places	placs	placies)
play	(playies	plays	plas)
rocket	(rocket	rockets	rocketts)
tomato	(tomaties	tomatos	tomatoes)
window	(windowes	windows	windas)

PHOTOCOPIABLE

■SCHOLASTIC
www.scholastic.co.uk

Illustrations © 1999, Tim Archibold.

Pluralisation

Random nouns

■ Take any text. It could be a story, a newspaper article, an advert or an information book. Read a chunk from it, finding the first **twenty** nouns. Write them in the correct column, then:

- If they are singular, write their plural form.
- If they are plural, write their singular form.

Remember, nouns can usually be changed from singular to plural

Singular	Plural

Illustrations © 1999, Tim Archibold.

Changes and word class

Objective

Use changes that can be made in words to identify word class.

Background knowledge

The various changes words can undergo and the relationships they form within a sentence can provide us with ways of recognising which words perform which function. To test for:

- **a noun:** can the word be pluralised? (Most nouns alter if they are changed from the singular to the plural.)
- **a verb:** can the word have its tense changed? (Most verbs alter as the tense of their phrase alters.)
- **an adjective:** does it modify the noun?
- **an adverb:** does it modify the verb?
- **a pronoun:** can the word be replaced by a noun?

Activities

These simple tests are bound to fail for certain words. For example, 'Paris' is a noun. Applying the plural test generates 'Parises'. The oddities remind us that the rules are only generalised ones, but they are ones that children can use, none the less.

- **Photocopiable page 117 'Wordsorts'**
Ask the children to test the words (using the rules given on the sheet) to highlight the different types of words used in the passage.
- **Photocopiable page 118 'Top ten parts'**
In this activity the children find lyrics from chosen songs and look at the language used. Pop songs often take on distinctive uses of language. An example from the not too distant past includes Des'ree's use of adjectives in the song *You Gotta Be*:
You gotta be bad, you gotta be bold
You gotta be wiser, you gotta be hard
You gotta be tough, you gotta be stronger
You gotta be cool, you gotta be calm
You gotta stay together…

- **Photocopiable page 119 'Your definitions'**
Children who have had experience of working with the various types of word (noun, verb, adjective and adverb) can, in this activity, set down their own definitions and examples. Their examples may include material from the previous activity or other current in-vogue material.

Further ideas

- **Parts in sentences:** Ask the children to try writing sentences that contain a noun, verb, adjective, adverb and pronoun. They can write the different types of words in different colours for easy identification.
- **Talkers:** Can the children think of anyone on television whose speech is particularly noticeable? It could be someone who whinges all the time or talks too quickly. They can listen to the speech of this person and see what types of word dominate their speech.
- **Adjective and adverb hunt:** The children can aim to find 100 adjectives or adverbs in texts around them. These could be on posters or notices, in newspaper and magazine headlines or in leaflets.

What's on the CD-ROM

On the CD-ROM you will find:
- Printable versions of all three photocopiable pages.
- Answers to 'Wordsorts'.
- Interactive version of 'Wordsorts'.

Changes and word class

Wordsorts

Here are some ways of detecting some of the different types of word in use:

If the word can change from a singular to a plural, it could be a **noun**.	If the word or phrase can be switched from one tense to another, it could be a **verb**.	If the word or phrase is adding to the meaning of the noun, it could be an **adjective**.	If the word or phrase is altering the meaning of the verb, it could be an **adverb**.	If a particular word can be replaced by a noun it could be a **pronoun**.

■ Using these rules, try to find the different types of word in this story. Circle the different types of word in different colours.

I know someone who went on a fishing trip. He took his old granddad with him. The boat was a rickety little one. The trip was great, but the weather started to get windy. The boat started rocking violently. They wondered if they should quickly turn back but Granddad said they should definitely carry on. He desperately wanted to catch a fish. Just then he foolishly leaned over the side and his false teeth fell into the water. He was really annoyed and this made him utterly determined to go on until they caught a fish.

After an hour on this rough sea it looked as if Granddad had finally caught a really big fish. But the fish quickly bit the fishing line and got away. The fish slowly bobbed up to the side of the boat and lifted its eyes out of the murky water. There, in its little mouth, they could see Granddad's false teeth.

Illustrations © 1999, Tim Archibold.

■SCHOLASTIC
www.scholastic.co.uk   **PHOTOCOPIABLE**   **Scholastic Literacy Skills**
                                              Grammar and punctuation: Year 4   **117**

Name:

Changes and word class

Top ten parts

■ Copy out the words to the chorus or the main lines from a current pop song.

■ Look at the language used. Look at the number of different types of word. Look at the way the words are arranged.
■ Write a few comments about the language of the pop song.

_____

_____

_____

_____

SCHOLASTIC
www.scholastic.co.uk

Illustrations © 1999, Tim Archibold.

Changes and word class

Your definitions

■ Write your own brief definitions of the different types of word, and give some examples for each one. The first one has been started for you.

■ Remember to note anything significant about the words – such as odd endings and changes.

■ Remember to include any interesting points from current usage or other languages you speak or have encountered.

Noun	Verb	Adjective	Adverb
the name you would call a thing			
Examples	**Examples**	**Examples**	**Examples**
the sun			

■SCHOLASTIC
www.scholastic.co.uk   **PHOTOCOPIABLE**   Scholastic Literacy Skills
Grammar and punctuation: Year 4   **119**

Choose the 'write' words

Objective

Apply, and develop the use of, rules for the changing of words in writing.

Writing focus

Through reflecting on their own writing, in this section children revisit some of the basic grammatical features such as tense changes and pluralisation.

Skills to writing

● Tense

Continually check the tenses in which different texts are written. As the children encounter a report text, a recount or persuasion, encourage them to reflect on why a particular tense suited the subject matter. Look out for interesting examples – a lot of jokes are written and said in the present tense: *A man walks into a bar…Ouch!*

● Focused revision

The children can focus on one grammatical rule, such as pluralisation, and read through their own writing to find examples of places where they have deployed, or should have deployed, the rules for making such changes. Children learn best from their own writing, and where they find examples of places they should have deployed a rule, they are learning to extend and improve their own skills.

● Roots and branches

When revising a single piece of work, ask the children to look for examples of where a root word has been changed throughout the text and to map the grammatical rules they have used to devise the variations. If, for example, they are writing about 'smell', they may use the plural to describe various *smells*, write how something *smelled* or how certain things are *smelly*. Encourage them to use their own writing to investigate where and why they have adopted a range of rules.

● The 'ing' thing

Children's narrative writing can be developed through encouraging them to explore 'ing' sentence starters and inserts. These can provide a means of developing the feelings of characters in a text. The 'ing' line is basically a line that starts with a word like 'thinking' or 'seeing', such as *Thinking he was not alone, Herbie turned around*, or *Seeing the door creak open, Herbie jumped through the window.* Such 'ing' lines can provide a way of stimulating the inclusion of interesting sentences that give an insight into why a character in a narrative behaves in a particular way.

● Superlative collection

Maintain a class collection of amazing facts about superlatives – the longest, biggest, heaviest and so on. Children love books of records and miscellanies of facts. Encourage a selective gathering of the most amazing ones – like the fact that the longest human hair ever grew to… you'll have to find that one out!

Activities

● Photocopiable page 122 'Story thinking'

This set of phrases can be used as story writing stimuli. They can form an initial stimulus for story writing or could be used by children who are planning a story to provide ideas of initial phrases they could use to generate some interesting sentences. Each of the phrases should engender some thought about what a character is thinking or feeling (see 'The "ing" thing' above). Once the children have used these, continue to promote the idea of how the 'ing' ending can be used to describe the process a character is experiencing in the middle of a section of narrative. The children can keep the examples in this activity in reserve for later use, or gather new examples from other verbs. Note that the 'she/he' alternatives present children with the chance to choose a character's gender.

● Photocopiable page 123 'My verbs'

Analysing their own writing and verb choice, this activity turns children back to their verbs with a view to coming up with some of the different forms that they can take. This is designed to be a quick activity, securing the children's knowledge of the various forms of the verbs they have already used, with the added possibility of exploring synonymous verbs they could also use. When doing this activity, children's starting point will depend on the verb form already used. If, in writing, they wrote *I walked to town*, then they enter the verb in the '-ed' column and work backwards to figure out 'walking' and 'walk'.

Write on

● Pop song

Ask the children to devise their own words to fit the chorus of the pop song they looked at on photocopiable page 118 'Top ten parts'. They can change the subject or vary the original. As they do this, ask them to look in a similar way at their own example – what classes of word have they used and how have they used them?

● Lies in stories

Following on from photocopiable page 110 'Liars', ask the children to write their own lying conversation, in which one character tries to best the other with progressively more comparative and superlative examples. Can they turn these into a short story or playscript? Remember how the whole mess that is the basis of the story of 'Rumpelstiltskin' started with a parent singing lying boasts about a daughter who could spin gold.

● Devise an advert

Jingle included, ask the children to devise their own advert for a made-up product. In it they can make full use of the future tense, promising what the product will do for its purchaser. Can they also use comparatives and superlatives to put their product ahead of its rivals?

● Class records

Create your own book of records for the class that could extend to the school. What stands as the length of the tallest card tower, the longest game of chess or the loudest sneeze? Once you start collecting them, these records grow and grow.

● Superlative quiz

Using comparatives and superlatives, the children can devise a quiz in which they can enter staff at their school or volunteer parents. Which is faster – a sneeze or a cheetah? What is the largest bird? Quizzes like this can throw up some surprising facts.

What's on the CD-ROM

On the CD-ROM you will find:
● Printable versions of both photocopiable pages.

Name:

Story thinking

■ Can you think of story ideas built around these phrases?

Realising I was not alone…	Losing friends…
Breaking a promise…	Thinking of running away…
Discovering the truth…	Seeing her/him for the first time…
Understanding why she/he did it…	Knowing what was really going on…

PHOTOCOPIABLE

Name:

Choose the 'write' words

My verbs

■ Use this chart to analyse the verbs you have used in writing.

The verb in my writing	Root verb	Other forms	Alternative verbs

Adverbs

Introduction

The focus for this chapter is on adverbs. Children look at the function they perform and the way they can be recognised. They also collect them and alter them.

Poster notes

Adjectives to adverbs (page 125)

The way adjectives can be turned into adverbs, looked at in 'The 'ly' suffix', provides a useful spelling lesson. However, it also helps children to identify adverbs. Once they have grasped this aspect of grammar, they will be able to turn adjectives they know into adverbs.

About the verb (page 126)

This poster gives the categories of adverb, with examples. It is a useful way of raising the questions around any action or happening – asking 'how did it happen?' or 'where and when?'.

In this chapter

Adverbs

Adjectives to adverbs

HAPPY

If the adjective ends in **y**,

HAPPILY

change the **y** to **i** before adding **ly**.

SLOW

WALKING SLOWLY

The usual way of making an adverb out of an adjective is to add **ly**.

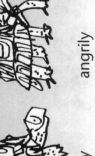

sleepily

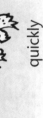

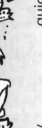

angrily

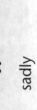
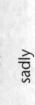
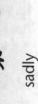
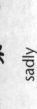

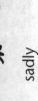

quickly

sadly

Illustrations © 2008 Tim Archibold.

Adverbs

About the verb

Adverbs tell us about verbs. They describe and give more detail about verbs. They can tell us...

How something happened	Where something happened	When something happened
For example *I ran quickly.* *Joe smiled happily.*	For example *I live over there.* *Sit on the other chair.*	For example *I'm going tomorrow.* *She flies upwards.*
The manner of the verb	The place of the verb	The time of the verb

Illustrations © 2008, Tim Archibold.

SCHOLASTIC
www.scholastic.co.uk

Identifying adverbs

Objective

Learn to identify adverbs, noticing where they occur in sentences and how they are used to modify the verbs.

Background knowledge

Adverbs modify verbs. They are the words or phrases in a sentence that say something about the action or happening described by the verb.

A sentence could just state: *Albert collapsed.*

It could say something about the manner in which he did this: *Albert suddenly collapsed.*

It could say where: *Albert suddenly collapsed on the floor.*

It could say when: *This morning Albert suddenly collapsed on the floor.*

These additions are adverbs – words modifying the verb.

Activities

Once children have a grasp of the function of verbs in a sentence they can begin to see how the adverbs modify the verbs. In these activities the children look for words and phrases that tell the reader or listener more about the verbs.

● **Photocopiable page 128 'How verbs happen'**
By looking at the words that modify the verbs in the sentences, the children should begin to understand the type of word or phrase that constitutes an adverb. Because the term 'adverb' covers a range of different types of modifier, the exercise has drawn on various ways in which a verb can be qualified. Stress to the children that they are looking for words or phrases that could be removed from the sentence without impairing the sense. They are also looking for anything that says something about the verb.

● **Photocopiable page 129 'Tell us more'**
This activity gives children an opportunity to experiment with their own production of adverbs. They could use poster page 125 for reference, as well as a list of adverbs compiled by the whole class.

● **Photocopiable page 130 'Action and manner'**
This is a game to play in a large group. Copy the sheet onto card and cut out the cards. Put the children into small teams of two or three. Place the cards face down in two piles. Each team takes turns to select an 'action' card and a 'manner' card. They then mime the action and the manner in which it is done. The other children have to guess the action and the manner. Stress that the actions are to be mimed, and that speaking is not allowed.

Further ideas

● **Adverb mimes:** The children can build on the 'Action and manner' activity by performing other actions in the manner of the adverbs on the cards. As their stock of adverbs develops they can create new 'manner' cards to modify the actions.

● **Comic pages:** Provide the children with comics and ask them to make a list of the pictorial representations of actions that they can see on the pages. They can then use adverbs to describe the manner in which each action is being done.

● **Modify it:** Invite the children to produce simple sentences such as the 'Albert collapsed' examples. Can they think of words that they could add to their starter phrase (for example, 'Albert slowly, quietly and foolishly collapsed'), gradually producing a lengthy sentence with a list of adverbs modifying the verb?

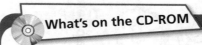 **What's on the CD-ROM**

On the CD-ROM you will find:
● Printable versions of all three photocopiable pages.
● Answers to 'How verbs happen'.
● Interactive version of 'How verbs happen'.

Name:

How verbs happen

■ Look at each of these examples and find the verbs (the actions or happenings) and the words that tell us about the verb. The first one has been done for you.

The boy quickly ran downstairs.		We played well on the muddy field.	
Verb	Words about the verb	Verb	Words about the verb
ran	quickly, downstairs		

Screw the bottle top on firmly after use.		I planted the seeds outside.	
Verb	Words about the verb	Verb	Words about the verb

Today we will sing pleasantly.		Listen carefully to the answerphone.	
Verb	Words about the verb	Verb	Words about the verb

PHOTOCOPIABLE ■SCHOLASTIC
www.scholastic.co.uk

Identifying adverbs

Tell us more

A sentence could say:

Lucy fell.

It could also say:

Today Lucy suddenly fell off her chair.

■ In the boxes below, draw pictures of people (or animals or monsters!) doing things. In the space underneath each of your drawings, write a sentence to explain the picture. Use an adverb to give a clear description of what is happening. The first one has been done for you.

Picture	Picture	Picture
Sentence Daniel wrote his story quickly.	Sentence	Sentence
Picture	Picture	Picture
Sentence	Sentence	Sentence

Illustrations © 1999, Tim Archibold.

Name:

Identifying adverbs

Action and manner

action taking a dog for a walk	manner slowly
action playing the piano	manner quickly
action pouring and eating breakfast cereal	manner happily
action mixing paints	manner pompously
action getting dressed	manner miserably
action meeting friends	manner sneakily
action catching a bus	manner nervously

The 'ly' suffix

Identify common adverbs with 'ly' suffix.

Background knowledge

Most adverbs are adverbs of manner. They explain how something was done. The majority of these adverbs are made by altering an adjective, either adding 'ly' to the end:

sad → *sadly*

or, if the adjective ends in 'y', changing the 'y' to 'i' then adding 'ly'.

happy → *happily*

   As with most spelling rules, there are exceptions to the rule, such as the word 'fast'. It can function as an adjective or it can remain the same to make an adverb:

fast talk

talk fast

   However, as spelling rules go, the 'ly' one acts as an important guide in working with adverbs.

Activities

As with any spelling rule, children need to learn the rule while also understanding the fact that there are exceptions. In these activities children encounter the 'ly' rule and also meet some of the exceptions. It is therefore important that they keep the overall definition of an adverb in mind and don't just rely on the 'ly' ending to discern which words fall into this class.

● **Photocopiable page 132 'Create the adverb'**
This activity asks children to apply the 'ly' rule to a range of adjectives. Before they start to work on the sheet, remind them of the function of an adjective and the important link between an action and the word (the adverb) that describes the action. Explain the activity by working on a few examples together, changing a phrase containing an adjective to a sentence using an adverb

formed from the adjective; encourage the children to think of a context in which a particular action could occur – for example, the phrase 'a soft step' could become the sentence *The burglar stepped softly*.

● **Photocopiable page 133 'Find the adverb'**
Review the nature and function of adverbs with the children undertaking this activity, and encourage them to refer to poster page 125. The sentences contain exceptions to the 'ly' rule alongside adverbs that conform to it. The exceptions may cause some discussion and debate.

● **Photocopiable page 134 'Making and using'**
Explain to the children that after reading the definitions of the adjectives and writing down the adverbs, they need to think of an action for each one that could be performed in a way that would merit the description given in the definition. They should then make up a sentence using the adverb.

Further ideas

● **Links:** Encourage the children to develop the habit of looking at adverbs to work out what the linked adjectives could be, and vice versa. In some cases adjectives do not have linked adverbs – for example, adjectives that describe colour, such as 'red'. What could it mean to perform an action 'redly'? What about the adjective 'fishy'? What sort of actions are done 'fishily'? Let the activity lead in to children inventing new adverbs.

● **Dictionary hunt:** Ask the children to search through a dictionary, listing unfamiliar adjectives, then finding or forming the linked adverbs.

What's on the CD-ROM

On the CD-ROM you will find:
● Printable versions of all three photocopiable pages.
● Answers to 'Find the adverb' and 'Making and using'.
● Interactive version of 'Find the adverb'.

Name:

The 'ly' suffix

Create the adverb

Adverbs are often made by adding **ly** to an adjective.

If the adjective ends in **y**, the **y** is changed to an **i** before adding the **ly**.

A quick paint.   She painted the wall quickly.

■ Write a short sentence for each of the actions. Add **ly** to the adjective (the bold word) to make your adverb.

Phrase with adjective	Use the adverb
an **immediate** cry	She cried immediately when she hurt herself.
a **sudden** flash	
an **angry** shout	
a **sweet** smile	
a **quick** jump	
a **strong** swim	
a **creepy** look	
a **quiet** whisper	
a **sharp** turn	

PHOTOCOPIABLE   ■SCHOLASTIC
www.scholastic.co.uk

The 'ly' suffix

Find the adverb

■ Look at the sentences and circle the adverb.
(Warning 1: some adverbs don't end in **ly**.)
(Warning 2: not every word that ends in **ly** is an adverb.)

■ Fill in the table to show the adverbs you found and the verbs they describe.

	Adverb	Verb it describes
A fly buzzed briskly around the room.	briskly	buzzed
Don't talk fast because it confuses me.		
You ran well and won the race.		
The dragon fought bravely with the monster.		
The plane flew low.		
Joe woke early and read his book.		
We quickly emptied the smelly old bottle.		
Dad accidentally dropped the telly.		
Lou pulled hard and my welly came off.		
We walked slowly into the temple.		
Leon slipped late into the silent classroom.		

Name:

The 'ly' suffix

Making and using

■ Look at the list of adjectives (describing words) and their dictionary definitions.
■ Make adverbs out of the adjectives by adding **ly**. If they end in a **y**, change the **y** to an **i** before adding **ly**.

■ Use the new adverb in a made-up sentence.

Adjective and definition	Adverb	Sentence
abominable awful, monstrous, horrible	→ abominably	The boy behaved abominably, throwing plates around the room.
bashful timid or shy, easily embarrassed	→	
cautious wary, taking care →		
entire complete, finished →		
gloomy miserable, with gloom	→	
humorous funny, making people laugh	→	
jealous wanting what another has	→	

PHOTOCOPIABLE

■SCHOLASTIC
www.scholastic.co.uk

Illustrations © 1999, Tim Archibold.

Classifying adverbs

Objective

Objective

Collect and classify examples of adverbs.

Background knowledge

The term 'adverb' covers a large group of words and phrases. These can be sorted according to the different functions they perform. The main groups of adverbs are those that explain:

- **Manner:** how a verb happened, for example: *He ran quickly.*
- **Place:** where a verb happened, for example: *He ran upstairs.*
- **Time:** when a verb happened, for example: *Later, he ran.*

These are the main categories of adverb, though there are others. There are also groups of adverbs that tend to modify particular verbs. There are verbs that particularly relate to the speed at which things happened (for example, *quickly, slowly*) and the attitude in which actions were performed (for example, *happily, miserably*).

Activities

Children can explore the groups of adverbs as a way of extending and developing their grasp of the function of adverbs. Through differentiating between different functions, children investigate various types of adverb. These activities look at the points at which adverbs are used and encourage the children to select the appropriate words to perform this function. (A note of caution: adverbs can be overused. The activities are intended to prompt children to use and understand adverbs, but there is a need to guard against overuse.)

- **Photocopiable page 136 'Sort the adverbs'**
Three broad categories of adverb are presented: adverbs of manner, time and place. Encourage the children to look at the adverb as an answer to a question about the action. What question could it be answering? Does the adverb answer 'how' something was done, or 'when' or 'where'?

- **Photocopiable page 137 'Adverb families'**
This activity focuses on adverbs that can be linked to certain types of action or happening. When the children have completed each 'spider', they are asked to write five sentences, each sentence incorporating an adverb from a different 'spider'. Children can follow this activity with a comparison of each other's words used to complete the 'spiders'.

- **Photocopiable page 138 'Adverb links'**
This is an investigative activity in which groups of three children explore the type of action and sentence they associate with a particular adverb. The emphasis is on the collation of their findings and, when looking at their results, the examination of the patterns in their outcomes. Let the children cut out their sentences, collecting those which incorporate the same adverbs together, and paste them down onto one large sheet.

Further ideas

- **How do you do that?:** Children can devise questions that are answerable using adverbs, such as *How do you walk into a classroom when you are late? How do you walk past a snarling dog?* They can put these to one another and seek out adverbs to provide answers.
- **Collecting adverbs:** As with many of the types of words looked at in this book, an enriching follow-up activity involves children collecting examples. Invite the children to make a list of new and interesting adverbial words and phrases as they read various texts.
- **Adverb associations:** The children can conduct a survey, setting the 'Adverb links' activity for other children and adults and comparing results. They can look at the field of meanings in which the adverbs feature, and perhaps adapt the activity to use new adverbs.

What's on the CD-ROM

On the CD-ROM you will find:
- Printable versions of all three photocopiable pages.
- Answers to 'Sort the adverbs'.
- Interactive version of 'Sort the adverbs'.

Name:

Classifying adverbs

Sort the adverbs

Some adverbs describe **manner**. They show **how** something happened.
He ran quickly.

Some adverbs describe **place**. They show **where** something happened.
He ran upstairs.

Some adverbs describe **time**. They show **when** something happened.
Later, he ran.

■ Look at the adverbs in the sentences. After each one, write either **manner**, **time** or **place**.

Adverb describes:

The bird sang **sweetly**. _____ manner _____

Let's go home **now**. _____

Come **here**. _____

Yesterday there was no school. _____

Put the chair **there**. _____

He ate **greedily**. _____

I will write **soon**. _____

We looked **everywhere** for new shoes. _____

Tiptoe **quietly** past the guard dog. _____

Stop that **immediately**! _____

Tuck your shirt **in**. _____

We cycled **quickly**. _____

He pulled **out** a plum. _____

It rained **miserably**. _____

The pirate buried the treasure **underground**. _____

We **sadly** said 'Goodbye' to our friend. _____

I am going swimming **today**. _____

Mum carried the baby **upstairs**. _____

Shout **loudly** so I can hear. _____

Classifying adverbs

Adverb families

■ Think of four different adverbs to describe each way of doing something.
Fill in the 'spiders'.

■ When you have completed the spiders, write a sentence using one adverb from
each completed 'spider'.

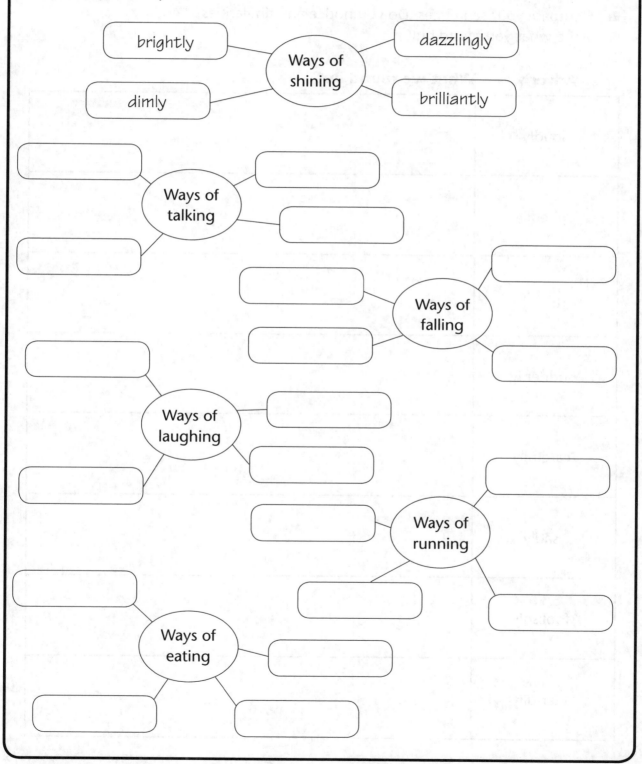

Name:

Classifying adverbs

Adverb links

■ There are eight different adverbs in the boxes below. Write eight sentences on a separate sheet of paper, using these adverbs. Use a different adverb in each one. Don't look at anyone else's in your group!

■ Compare your sentences. Do you notice any similarities?
■ Write what you found out.

Adverb	What we found out
loudly	
greedily	
quietly	
suddenly	
carefully	
sadly	
foolishly	
fearfully	

Changing adverbs

Investigate the effects of substituting adverbs in particular contexts.

Background knowledge

Selection is an important part of the way we use language. There are a vast number of possible adverbs from which the speaker or writer selects the one to use. Part of the scope for selection of adverbs lies in the fact that most sentences could get by perfectly well without them. Adverbs add information about the verb. Sometimes this is essential. On the other hand, as mentioned previously, adverbs can be overused, particularly certain adverbs of degree such as 'really' (as in *I'll tell you what I want, what I really, really want*) and 'very'. If something was silly does it make much difference to say it was *very silly* or *very, very silly*? (Teachers take note.)

For this reason it is interesting to look at the selection of adverbs and the way in which apposite words are chosen for the right context.

Activities

There are no right or wrong answers in these activities. Each activity offers children the possibility of a range of answers. It is therefore important that you make time for reflection, analysis and more than one 'conclusion'. Through looking at various types of text, children focus on the context as a way into understanding and selecting adverbs.

- **Photocopiable page 140 'Suggested adverbs'**
The two stages to this activity involve, firstly, children devising adverbs to be used in the sentences and secondly, comparing their results. This should demonstrate the idea that we can select and alter a selection of adverbs for a particular sentence. It also provides an opportunity for the children to experience having a selection of possible words to fit into a sentence and choosing the best one.

- **Photocopiable page 141 'Possible adverbs'**
In filling in the word spaces in this activity, the children will need to look at the context and the type of adverb most appropriate to it. Again there may be varied results worth comparing. Look out for interesting combinations. This is the sort of activity that shows that, when encouraged, children can be far more daring with language than adults. The children are encouraged to suggest three possibilities for each space. Can they suggest more?

- **Photocopiable page 142 'Adverbs in action'**
This activity looks at a short extract from the book *It's Too Frightening For Me!* by Shirley Hughes. The children should have some idea of the context before they read it. It is taken from an early point in the story which is full of suspense. Explain that prior to seeing the girl's face at the window of the gloomy house in which nobody ever comes or goes (except for a big black cat), Jim and Arthur had heard 'ghostly screams'. It is important to stress that suggesting alternative adverbs does not involve improving the text. It is merely to appreciate the way that descriptions of actions can be enhanced by a variety of adverbs, all of equal merit but different in their effect.

Further ideas

- **Adverb strings:** The children can look at the addition of adverb to adverb to make a string of words modifying the verb. For example: *Slowly, calmly and steadily, the tightrope walker set off* uses a string of adverbs to describe an action occurring. The children may be able to make similar strings by applying questions such as *How did it happen? When did it happen? Where did it happen?* to a verb.

What's on the CD-ROM

On the CD-ROM you will find:
- Printable versions of all three photocopiable pages.
- Interactive versions of 'Suggested adverbs' and 'Possible adverbs'.

Changing adverbs

Suggested adverbs

■ Read the following sentences and suggest an adverb that could be inserted in each one. Write them on the lines.

The slug slithered ——————— up the window.

A star shone ——————— in the sky.

The car chugged ——————— to a halt.

The coach shouted ——————— at the footballers.

——————— , a firework shot into the sky.

The bus was leaving so I ran ———————.

The children played ——————— in the playground.

The ball bounced ——————— and went over the fence.

When they are angry teachers talk ———————.

■ List **five** adverbs you used in some of the sentences.
■ For each word, find a different adverb you could have put in its place.
■ Find a different adverb someone else in your class used.
■ Circle the adverb that you think works best.

	Adverb	My alternative adverb	A friend's adverb
1			
2			
3			
4			
5			

Illustrations © 1999, Tim Archibold.

Changing adverbs

Possible adverbs

■ Read the sentences and write three adverbs that could fit in the spaces. You can use adverbs from the list at the foot of the page. Try using each adverb once.

The dog slept _____ in his basket, snoozing and snoring. The burglar

moved _____ up the creaking stairs. But _____ the dog

woke up. The dog barked _____ at the burglar. The dog _____

chased the burglar. The burglar climbed _____ up the tree. The dog

growled _____ at the bottom of the tree. The burglar _____

edged _____ along the branch, trying to reach over

the wall. _____ it snapped.

peacefully	carefully	loudly	hastily	anxiously
dreamily	annoyingly	fiercely	speedily	viciously
pleasantly	suddenly	madly	doggedly	nastily
sneakily	immediately	quickly	hurriedly	cautiously
quietly	gently	fearfully	keenly	slowly

Name:

Changing adverbs

Adverbs in action

■ Look at this passage from Shirley Hughes's book *It's Too Frightening For Me!* Jim and Arthur live near an eerie house. The previous day, they have seen a strange girl's face looking out from a window.

Next day they watched from the wall for a long time, but no face appeared. Then Jim noticed a basement door at the bottom of a flight of steps, where the shutter had slipped and a glass pane was broken.

    Jim slithered down into the yard and tried the door. It opened! Putting his finger to his lips, Jim made signs to Arthur to stay where he was. Then he disappeared into the house.

    Poor Arthur! He badly wanted to run home, but he couldn't desert his brother. After a long while, he too climbed softly down into the yard and, trembling all over, crept in through the basement door to look for Jim.

■ Some verbs are in the first column. Find them in the story, then find their adverbs (words that say something about the verb). Think of some different adverbs you could use instead of the ones used in the story.

Verbs	Adverbs in the story	Adverbs that could have been used
watched		
slithered		
stay		
wanted		
run		
climbed		
crept		

PHOTOCOPIABLE   **■SCHOLASTIC**
www.scholastic.co.uk

Text and illustration © 1977, Shirley Hughes.

Incredibly useful adverbs

Objective

Develop the use of adverbs in writing.

Writing focus

These activities guide children in applying their understanding of adverbs in their writing. The focus is on the meaning and effect of adverbs, and the way they modify verbs.

Skills to writing

● **How?**

The question 'How?' is the key to working with adverbs. Children should have that at the forefront of their minds when considering adverbs in their own writing. Someone did something – but how did they do it? In any text children may find an adverb relating how an action was done. If they don't, they could still infer or imagine this. No adverb describes how the Wild Things called to Max in *Where the Wild Things Are*, but we can imagine – though it's an interesting one to consider. Was it 'angrily' or 'desperately'?

● **Emotional adverbs**

Look for the emotion behind the adverb. Many adverbs imply a feeling on the part of the subject of the verb. If someone opened the door 'quickly' they have some motive for their speed; if they do it 'gloomily' we may wonder what's up.

● **Adverbial phrases**

Adverbial phrases make up some interesting examples of language use that the children can adapt in their own writing. Many conjure up an image, sometimes using a simile, such as *He ran like lightning*. Watch out for them and draw children's attention to them, always making the link – how does the subject used in the image link to the original action?

● **Don't overdo it**

Don't overdo adverbs. Once children have learned adverbs it's not uncommon to read narrative writing in which every single verb is modified, to an unnecessary degree. Emphasise to the children that they need to be selective. In one sentence they should consider which verb could really do with an adverb.

● **Moving adverbs**

Try adverbs in different places. Take the sentence
Joe opened the window.
It could be:
Suddenly, Joe opened the window.
Joe suddenly opened the window.
Joe opened the window, suddenly.

Ask the children to look for the one that best suits a particular context. Can they say what it is that makes the difference between three sentences like this? Does one have a more sudden start? Does one feel more like we're with the character, rather than being surprised by him? It's subjective, but children will have their views.

● **Non-fiction adverbs**

Focus on the use of adverbs in non-fiction writing, particularly in the writing of explanation texts. Here the verbs present the stages in a process. As the children write up their findings from a scientific process, they should be encouraged to use adverbs to vividly present how the things they have done looked, smelled, moved and sounded.

Activities

● **Photocopiable page 145 'Improving the story's heart'**

The story planner on this photocopiable sheet delves into the middle of a narrative and asks children to consider some of the actions that will fill out this section. The middle of a narrative is often the flabbiest part of a child's writing so it pays to emphasise the planning of this section. Having thought of the main verbs that will underpin the story, children can gather adverbs that will enrich the language they use to depict these moments in their writing.

● **Photocopiable page 146 'Ways of doing'**

As a way of unpicking the varied ways in which the children could modify the verbs in their writing, this photocopiable sheet asks them to think through some of the verbs they encountered and worked with in Chapter 1 and consider some of the varied ways in which these actions could be undertaken. Once they have done this they could draft up some examples of the various verbs and adverbs in sentences, remembering that they can change the word order, as shown above.

As the children do this they need to keep the question 'How?' in the forefront of their minds.

Write on

● **Settings**

Children can work in groups of three to devise a map of a setting where a story could take place. It could be a scary funfair or a pirate ship. As they devise their setting they can fill it with various hazards and annotate these with adverbs, indicating how a character would move through that setting. How would someone cross the creaky rope bridge? How would they eat the chocolate at the chocolate river?

● **Adverb mapping**

Children can use adverbs as a way of extending their planning and mapping out of narrative writing. As they plan a storyline they can consider how the various actions were done. This provides a useful way of engaging children with the emotions of the characters in their story. They will often envisage a basic action, such as 'a scared character running'. However, if they think of this as 'a scared character running fearfully' they have started to work through the emotions that are featuring in their narrative.

● **Inner life**

As children think through their writing of recounts and stories, ask them to draw thought bubbles. In these they can jot down the feelings of the characters and, in so doing, gain a greater insight into why characters perform their actions. If a character slams a door and they note this is done 'because he is angry', the resultant sentence could be *He angrily slammed the door*.

● **Movements**

Re-read some stories with the children. Ask them to look out for some of the actions that are undertaken and the ways in which they are done. Two areas to focus on are exploring the ways in which characters speak and the ways in which they move. Both of these can enrich children's word-stock for their writing.

What's on the CD-ROM

On the CD-ROM you will find:
● Printable versions of both photocopiable pages.

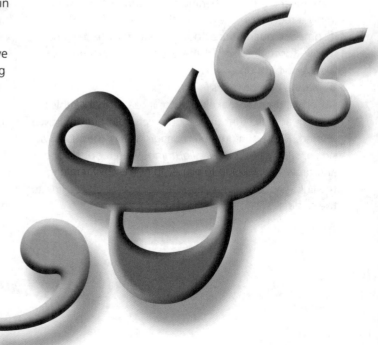

Incredibly useful adverbs

Improving the story's heart

■ Look at the verbs that will propel along the middle section of your story and try finding some adverbs that modify them.

Verbs	Adverbs describing the verbs

Name:

Incredibly useful adverbs

Ways of doing

■ Look at these different activities. How could you do each one? Think of adverbs to describe each one and write them in the boxes.

Ways of thinking	Ways of finding
_____ _____ _____ _____	_____ _____ _____ _____

Ways of finding	Ways of finding
_____ _____ _____ _____	_____ _____ _____ _____

Ways of finding	Ways of finding
_____ _____ _____ _____	_____ _____ _____ _____

Subject knowledge

1. Preliminary notes about grammar

Grammar involves the way in which words of different types are combined into sentences. The explanatory sections that follow will include definitions of types of word along with notes on how they are combined into sentences.

Three preliminary points about grammar:

- Function is all-important. Where a word is placed in relation to another word is crucial in deciding whether it is functioning as a verb or a noun. For example, the word 'run' will often be thought of as a verb. However, in a sentence like *They went for a run*, the word functions as a noun and the verb is 'went'.
- There are some consistencies in the way spelling is linked to grammar. For example, words like 'play' and 'shout' have the '-ed' ending to make past tense verbs, 'played' and 'shouted'. Adjectives like 'quick' and 'slow' take a '-ly' ending to make adverbs like 'quickly' and 'slowly'. There are exceptions to these rules but such consistencies can still prove useful when it comes to understanding the grammar of sentences.
- Nothing is sacred in language. Rules change over time; the double negative has gained currency and regional variation in accent and dialect is now far more valued than has been the case in the past. The rules of grammar that follow are subject to change as the language we use lives and grows.

2. Words and functions

Grammar picks out the functions of words. The major classes or types of word in the English language are:

Noun

The name of something or someone, including concrete things, such as 'dog' or 'tree', and abstract things, such as 'happiness' or 'fear'.

Pronoun

A word that replaces a noun. The noun 'John' in *John is ill* can be replaced by a pronoun 'he', making *He is ill*.

Verb

A word that denotes an action or a happening. In the sentence *I ate the cake* the verb is 'ate'. These are sometimes referred to as 'doing' words.

Adjective

A word that modifies a noun. In the phrase *the little boat* the adjective 'little' describes the noun 'boat'.

Adverb

A word that modifies a verb. In the phrase *he slowly walked* the adverb is 'slowly'.

Preposition

A word or phrase that shows the relationship of one thing to another. In the phrase *the house beside the sea* the preposition 'beside' places the two nouns in relation to each other.

Conjunction

A word or phrase that joins other words and phrases. A simple example is the word 'and' that joins nouns in *Snow White and Doc and Sneezy*.

Article

The indefinite articles in English are 'a' and 'an' and the definite article is 'the'. Articles appear before nouns and denote whether the noun is specific (*give me the book*) or not (*give me a book*).

Interjection

A word or phrase expressing or exclaiming an emotion, such as 'Oh!' and 'Aaargh!'
The various word types can be found in the following example sentences:

Lou	saw	his	new	house	from	the	train.
noun	verb	pronoun	adjective	noun	preposition	article	noun
Yeow!	I	hit	my	head	on	the	door.
interjection	pronoun	verb	pronoun	noun	preposition	article	noun
Amir	sadly	lost	his	bus fare	down	the	drain.
noun	adverb	verb	pronoun	noun	preposition	article	noun
Give	Jan	a	good	book	for	her	birthday.
verb	noun	article	adjective	noun	conjunction	pronoun	noun

The pages that follow provide more information on these word classes.

Nouns

There are four types of noun in English.

> A **noun** is the name of someone or something.

Common nouns are general names for things. For example, in the sentence *I fed the dog*, the noun 'dog' could be used to refer to any dog, not to a specific one. Other examples include 'boy', 'country', 'book', 'apple'.

Proper nouns are the specific names given to identify things or people. In a phrase like *Sam is my dog* the word 'dog' is the common noun but 'Sam' is a proper noun because it refers to and identifies a specific dog. Other examples include 'the Prime Minister', 'Wales' and 'Amazing Grace'.

Collective nouns refer to a group of things together, such as 'a flock (of sheep)' or 'a bunch (of bananas)'.

Abstract nouns refer to things that are not concrete, such as an action, a concept, an event, quality or state. Abstract nouns like 'happiness' and 'fulfilment' refer to ideas or feelings which are uncountable; others, such as 'hour', 'joke' and 'quantity' are countable.

Nouns can be singular or plural. To change a singular to a plural the usual rule is to add 's'. This table includes other rules to bear in mind, however:

If the singular ends in:	Rule	Examples
'y' after a consonant	Remove 'y', add 'ies'	party → parties
'y' after a vowel	add 's'	donkey → donkeys
'o' after a consonant	add 'es'	potato → potatoes
'o' after a vowel	add 's'	video → videos
an 's' sound such as 's', 'sh', 'x', 'z'	add 'es'	kiss → kisses dish → dishes
a 'ch' sound such as 'ch' or 'tch'	add 'es'	watch → watches church → churches

Pronouns

There are different classes of pronoun. The main types are:

Personal pronouns refer to people or things, such as 'I', 'you', 'it'. The personal pronouns distinguish between subject and object case ('I/me', 'he/him', 'she/her', 'we/us', 'they/them' and the archaic 'thou/thee').

> A **pronoun** is a word that stands in for a noun.

Reflexive pronouns refer to people or things that are also the subject of the sentence. In the sentence *You can do this yourself* the pronoun 'yourself' refers to 'you'. Such pronouns end with '-self' or '-selves'. Other examples include 'myself', 'themselves'.

Possessive pronouns identify people or things as belonging to a person or thing. For example, in the sentence *The book is hers* the possessive pronoun 'hers' refers to 'the book'. Other examples include 'its' and 'yours'. Note that possessive pronouns never take an apostrophe.

Relative pronouns link relative clauses to their nouns. In the sentence *The man who was in disguise sneaked into the room* the relative clause 'who was in disguise' provides extra information about 'the man'. This relative clause is linked by the relative pronoun 'who'. Other examples include 'whom', 'which' and 'that'.

Interrogative pronouns are used in questions. They refer to the thing that is being asked about. In the question *What is your name?* and *Where is the book?* the pronouns 'what' and 'where' stand for the answers – the name and the location of the book.

Demonstrative pronouns are pronouns that 'point'. They are used to show the relation of the speaker to an object. There are four demonstrative pronouns in English 'this', 'that', 'these', 'those' used as in *This is my house* and *That is your house*. They have specific uses, depending upon the position of the object to the speaker:

	Near to speaker	**Far away from speaker**
Singular	this	that
Plural	these	those

Indefinite pronouns stand in for an indefinite noun. The indefinite element can be the number of elements or the nature of them but they are summed up in ambiguous pronouns such as 'any', 'some' or 'several'. Other examples are the pronouns that end with '-body', '-one' and '-thing', such as 'somebody', 'everyone' and 'anything'.

Person

Personal, reflexive and possessive pronouns can be in the first, second or third person.
- First-person pronouns ('I', 'we') involve the speaker or writer.
- Second-person pronouns ('you') refer to the listener or reader.
- Third-person pronouns refer to something other than these two participants in the communication ('he', 'she', 'it', 'they').

The person of the pronoun will agree with particular forms of verbs: 'I like'/'she likes'.

Verbs

The **tense** of a verb places a happening in time. The main three tenses are the present, past and future.

To express an action that will take place in the future, verbs appear with 'will' or 'shall' (or 'going to'). The regular past tense is formed by the addition of the suffix '-ed', although some of the most common verbs in English (the 'strong' verbs) have irregular past tenses.

> A **verb** is a word that denotes an action or a happening.

Present tense (happening now)	**Past tense (happened in past)**	**Future tense (to happen in future)**
am, say, find, kick	was, said, found, kicked	will be, will say, shall find, shall kick

Continuous verbs

The present participle form of a verb is used to show a continuous action. Whereas a past tense like 'kicked' denotes an action that happened ('I kicked'), the present participle denotes the action as happening and continuing as it is described (*I was kicking*, the imperfect tense, or *I am kicking*, the present continuous). There is a sense in these uses of an action that has not ended.

The present participle usually ends in '-ing', such as 'walking', 'finding', and continuous verbs are made with a form of the verb 'be', such as 'was' or 'am': *I was running* and *I am running*.

Auxiliary verbs

Auxiliary verbs 'help' other verbs – they regularly accompany full verbs, always preceding them in a verb phrase. The auxiliary verbs in English can be divided into three categories:

Primary verbs are used to indicate the timing of a verb, such as 'be', 'have' or 'did' (including all their variations such as 'was', 'were', 'has', 'had' and so on). These can be seen at work in verb forms like *I was watching a film*, *He has finished eating*, *I didn't lose my keys*.

Modal verbs indicate the possibility of an action occurring or the necessity of it happening, such as *I might watch a film*, *I should finish eating* and *I shouldn't lose my keys*.

The modal verbs in English are: 'would', 'could', 'might', 'should', 'can', 'will', 'shall', 'may', and 'must'. These verbs never function on their own as main verbs. They always act as auxiliaries helping other verbs.

Marginal modals, namely 'dare', 'need', 'ought to' and 'used to'. These act as modals, such as in the sentences *I dared enter the room*, *You need to go away* and *I ought to eat my dinner*, but they can also act as main verbs, as in *I need cake*.

Adjectives

The main function of adjectives is to define quality or quantity. Examples of the use of descriptions of quality include 'good story', 'sad day' and 'stupid dog'. Examples of the use of descriptions of quantity include 'some stories', 'ten days' and 'many dogs'.

> An **adjective** is a word that modifies a noun.

Adjectives can appear in one of three different degrees of intensity. In the table on page 152 it can be seen that there are '-er' and '-est' endings that show an adjective is comparative or superlative, though, as can be seen, there are exceptions. The regular comparative is formed by the addition of the suffix '-er' to shorter words and 'more' to longer words ('kind/kinder', 'beautiful/more beautiful'). The regular superlative is formed by the addition of the suffix '-est' to shorter words and 'most' to longer words. Note, however, that some common adjectives have irregular comparatives and superlatives.

Nominative	Comparative	Superlative
The nominative is the plain form that describes a noun.	The comparative implies a comparison between the noun and something else.	The superlative is the ultimate degree of a particular quality.
Examples long small big fast bad good far	**Examples** longer smaller bigger faster worse better farther/further	**Examples** longest smallest biggest fastest worst best farthest/furthest

Adverbs

Adverbs provide extra information about the time, place or manner in which a verb happened.

> An **adverb** is a word that modifies a verb.

Manner Provides information about the manner in which the action was done.	Ali *quickly* ran home. The cat climbed *fearfully* up the tree.
Time Provides information about the time at which the action occurred.	*Yesterday* Ali ran home. *Sometimes* the cat climbed up the tree.
Place Provides information about where the action took place.	*Outside* Ali ran home. *In the garden* the cat climbed up the tree.

Variations in the degree of intensity of an adverb are indicated by other adjectives such as 'very', 'rather', 'quite' and 'somewhat'. Comparative forms include 'very quickly', 'rather slowly', and 'most happily'.

The majority of single-word adverbs are made by adding '-ly' to an adjective: 'quick/quickly', 'slow/slowly' and so on.

Prepositions

Prepositions show how nouns or pronouns are positioned in relation to other nouns and pronouns in the same sentence. This can often be the location of one thing in relation to another in space, such as 'on', 'over', 'near'; or time, such as 'before', 'after'.

Prepositions are usually placed before a noun. They can consist of one word (*The cat* in *the tree...*), two words (*The cat* close to *the gate...*) or three (*The cat* on top of *the roof...*).

> A **preposition** is a word or phrase that shows the relationship of one thing to another.

Connectives

The job of a connective is to maintain cohesion through a piece of text.

> A **connective** is a word or phrase that links clauses or sentences.

Connectives can be:

- Conjunctions – connect clauses within one sentence.
- Connecting adverbs – connect ideas in separate sentences.

Conjunctions

Conjunctions are a special type of connective. There are two types: coordinating or subordinating.

Coordinating conjunctions connect clauses of equal weight. For example: *I like cake and I like tea.* Coordinating conjunctions include: 'and', 'but', 'or' and 'so'.

Subordinating conjunctions are used where the clauses of unequal weight, they begin a subordinate clause. For example: *The dog barked because he saw the burglar.* Subordinating conjunctions include: 'because', 'when', 'while', 'that', 'although', 'if', 'until', 'after', before' and 'since'.

Name of conjunction	Nature of conjunction	Examples
Addition	One or more clause together	We had our tea *and* went out to play.
Opposition	One or more clauses in opposition	I like coffee *but* my brother hates it. It could rain *or* it could snow.
Time	One or more clauses connected over time	Toby had his tea *then* went out to play. The bus left *before* we reached the stop.
Cause	One or more clauses causing or caused by another	I took a map *so that* we wouldn't get lost. We got lost *because* we had the wrong map.

Connecting adverbs

The table below provides the function of the adverbs and examples of the type of words used for that purpose.

Addition	'also', 'furthermore', 'moreover', 'likewise'
Opposition	'however', 'never the less', 'on the other hand'
Time	'just then', 'meanwhile', 'later'
Result	'therefore', 'as a result'
Reinforcing	'besides', 'anyway'
Explaining	'for example', 'in other words'
Listing	'first of all', 'finally'

3. Understanding sentences

Types of sentence

The four main types of sentence are declarative, interrogative, imperative and exclamatory. The function of a sentence has an effect on the word order; imperatives, for example, often begin with a verb.

Sentences: Clauses and complexities

Phrases

A phrase is a set of words performing a grammatical function. In the sentence *The little, old, fierce dog brutally chased the sad and fearful cat*, there are three distinct units performing grammatical functions. The first phrase in this sentence essentially names the dog and provides descriptive information. This is a noun phrase, performing the job of a noun – 'the little, old, fierce dog'. To do this the phrase uses adjectives.

Sentence type	Function	Examples
Declarative	Makes a statement	The house is down the lane. Joe rode the bike.
Interrogative	Asks a question	Where is the house? What is Joe doing?
Imperative	Issues a command or direction	Turn left at the traffic lights. Get on your bike!
Exclamatory	Issues an interjection	Wow, what a mess! Oh no!

The important thing to look out for is the way in which words build around a key word in a phrase. So here the words 'little', 'old' and 'fierce' are built around the word 'dog'. In examples like these, 'dog' is referred to as the **headword** and the adjectives are termed **modifiers**. Together, the modifier and headword make up the noun phrase. Modifiers can also come after the noun, as in *The little, old, fierce dog that didn't like cats brutally chased the sad and fearful cat*. In this example 'little, 'old' and 'fierce' are **premodifiers** and the phrase 'that didn't like cats' is a **postmodifier**.

Phrase type	Examples
Noun phrase	The *little, old fierce dog* didn't like cats. She gave him *a carefully and colourfully covered book*.
Verb phrase	The dog *had been hiding* in the house. The man *climbed through* the window without a sound.
Adjectival phrase	The floor was *completely clean*. The floor was *so clean you could eat your dinner off it*.
Adverbial phrase	I finished my lunch *very slowly indeed*. *More confidently than usual*, she entered the room.
Prepositional phrase	The cat sat *at the top of* the tree. The phone rang *in the middle of* the night.

The noun phrase is just one of the types of phrase that can be made.

Notice that phrases can appear within phrases. A noun phrase like 'carefully and colourfully covered book' contains the adjectival phrase 'carefully and colourfully covered'. This string of words forms the adjectival phrase in which the words 'carefully' and 'colourfully' modify the adjective 'covered'. Together these words, 'carefully and colourfully covered', modify the noun 'book', creating a distinct noun phrase. This is worth noting as it shows how the boundaries between phrases can be blurred – a fact that can cause confusion unless borne in mind!

Clauses

Clauses are units of meaning included within a sentence, usually containing a verb and other elements linked to it. *The burglar ran* is a clause containing the definite article, noun and verb; *The burglar quickly ran from the little house* is also a clause that adds an adverb, preposition and adjective. The essential element in a clause is the verb. Clauses look very much like small sentences, indeed sentences can be constructed of just one clause: *The burglar hid, I like cake*.

Sentences can also be constructed out of a number of clauses linked together: *The burglar ran and I chased him because he stole my cake*. This sentence contains three clauses: 'The burglar ran', 'I chased him', 'he stole my cake'.

Clauses and phrases: the difference

Clauses include participants in an action denoted by a verb. Phrases, however, need not necessarily contain a verb. These phrases make little sense on their own: 'without a sound', 'very slowly indeed'. They work as part of a clause.

Simple, compound and complex sentences

The addition of clauses can make complex or compound sentences.

Simple sentences are made up of one clause, for example: *The dog barked, Sam was scared*.

Compound sentences are made up of clauses added to clauses. In compound sentences each of the clauses is of equal value; no clause is dependent on another. An example of a compound sentence is: *The dog barked and the parrot squawked*. Both these clauses are of equal importance: 'The dog barked', 'the parrot squawked'. Other compound sentences include, for example: *I like coffee and I like chocolate, I like coffee, but I don't like tea*.

Complex sentences are made up of a main clause with a subordinate clause or clauses. Subordinate clauses make sense in relation to the main clause. They say something about it and are dependent upon it, such as in the sentences: *The dog barked because he saw a burglar; Sam was scared so he phoned the police*.

In both these cases the subordinate clause ('he saw a burglar', 'he phoned the police') is elaborating on the main clause. They explain why the dog barked or why Sam was scared and, in doing so, are subordinate to those actions. The reader needs to see the main clauses to fully appreciate what the subordinate ones are stating.

Subject and object

The **subject** of a sentence or clause is the agent that performs the action denoted by the verb – *Shaun threw the ball*. The **object** is the agent to which the verb is done – 'ball'. It could be said that the subject does the verb to the object (a simplification but a useful one). The simplest type of sentence is known as the SVO (subject–verb–object) sentence (or clause), as in *You lost your way*, *I found the book* and *Lewis met Chloe*.

The active voice and the passive voice

These contrast two ways of saying the same thing:

Active voice	Passive voice
I found the book. Megan met Ben. The cow jumped over the moon.	The book was found by me. Ben was met by Megan. The moon was jumped over by the cow.

The two types of clause put the same subject matter in a different voice. Passive clauses are made up of a subject and verb followed by an agent.

The book	was found by	me.
subject	verb	agent
Ben	was met by	Megan.
subject	verb	agent

Sentences can be written in the active or the passive voice. A sentence can be changed from the active to the passive voice by:

- moving the subject to the end of the clause
- moving the object to the start of the clause
- changing the verb or verb phrase by placing a form of the verb 'be' before it (as in 'was found')
- changing the verb or verb phrase by placing 'by' after it.

In passive clauses the agent can be deleted, either because it does not need mentioning or because a positive choice is made to omit it. Texts on science may leave out the agent, with sentences such as *The water is added to the salt and stirred*.

4. Punctuation

Punctuation provides marks within sentences that guide the reader. Speech doesn't need punctuation (and would sound bizarre if it included noises for full stops and so on). In speech, much is communicated by pausing, changing tone and so on. In writing, the marks within and around a sentence provide indications of when to pause, when something is being quoted and so on.

Punctuation	Uses	Examples
A	**Capital letter** 1. Starts a sentence. 2. Indicates proper nouns. 3. Emphasises certain words.	All I want is cake. You can call me Al. I want it TOMORROW!
.	**Full stop** Ends sentences that are not questions or exclamations.	This is a sentence.
?	**Question mark** Ends a sentence that is a question.	Is this a question?
!	**Exclamation mark** Ends a sentence that is an exclamation.	Don't do that!
" " ' '	**Quotation (speech) marks (or inverted commas)** Encloses direct speech. Can be double or single.	"Help me," the man yelled. 'Help me,' the man yelled.
,	**Comma** 1. Places a pause between clauses within a sentence. 2. Separates items in a list. 3. Separates adjectives in a series. 4. Completely encloses clauses inserted in a sentence. 5. Marks speech from words denoting who said them.	We were late, although it didn't matter. You will need eggs, butter and flour. I wore a long, green, frilly skirt. We were, after we had rushed to get there, late for the film. 'Thank you,' I said.
—	**Hyphen** Connects elements of certain words.	Co-ordinator, south-west.
:	**Colon** 1. Introduces lists (including examples).	To go skiing these are the main items you will need: a hat, goggles, gloves and sunscreen.
	2. Introduces summaries.	We have learned the following on the ski slope: do a snow plough to slow down…
	3. Introduces (direct) quotations.	My instructor always says: 'Bend those knees.'
	4. Introduces a second clause that expands or illustrates the meaning of the first.	The snow hardened: it turned into ice.

Punctuation	Uses	Examples
;	**Semicolon** 1. Separates two closely linked clauses, and shows there is a link between them. 2. Separates items in a complex list.	On Tuesday, the bus was late; the train was early. You can go by aeroplane, train and taxi; Channel tunnel train, coach, then a short walk; or aeroplane and car.
'	**Apostrophe of possession** Denotes the ownership of one thing by another (see page 159).	This is Mona's scarf. These are the teachers' books.
'	**Apostrophe of contraction** Shows the omission of a letter(s) when two (or occasionally more) words are contracted.	Don't walk on the grass.
...	**Ellipsis** 1. Shows the omission of words. 2. Indicates a pause.	The teacher moaned, 'Look at this floor... a mess... this class...' Lou said: 'I think I locked the door... no, hang on, did I?'
( )	**Brackets** Contains a parenthesis – a word or phrase added to a sentence to give a bit more information.	The cupboard (which had been in my family for years) was broken.
—	**Dash** 1. Indicates additional information, with more emphasis than a comma. 2. Indicates a pause, especially for effect at the end of a sentence. 3. Contains extra information (used instead of brackets).	She is a teacher – and a very good one too. We all know what to expect – the worst. You finished that job – and I don't know how – before the deadline.

Adding an apostrophe of possession

The addition of an apostrophe can create confusion. The main thing to look at is the noun – ask:

- Is it singular or plural?
- Does it end in an 's'?

If the noun is singular and doesn't end in 's', you add an apostrophe and an 's', for example: Indra's house the firefighter's bravery	**If the noun is singular and ends in 's'**, you add an apostrophe and an 's', for example: the bus's wheels Thomas's pen
If the noun is plural and doesn't end in 's', you add an apostrophe and an 's', for example: the women's magazine the geese's flight	**If the noun is plural and ends in 's'**, you add an apostrophe but don't add an 's', for example: the boys' clothes the dancers' performance

Further reading

Carter, R; Goddard, A; Reah, D; Sanger, K; Bowring, K (2001) *Working with Texts: A Core Book for Language Analysis* (second edition), Routledge

Crystal, D (2004) *Rediscover Grammar* (second edition), Longman

Crystal, D (2003) *The Cambridge Encyclopedia of the English Language* (second edition), Cambridge University Press
A big volume but very accessible, covering many areas of English including grammar, punctuation and dialect. Filled with interesting asides and examples from sources as varied as Shakespeare to Monty Python.

Hurford, JR (1994) *Grammar: A Student's Guide*, Cambridge University Press
An excellent text, setting out basic guidelines on the workings of grammar.

Sealey, A (1996) *Learning About Language: Issues for Primary Teachers*, Open University Press
A more theoretical work that presents some of the issues and arguments surrounding knowledge about language.

■SCHOLASTIC

Also available in this series:

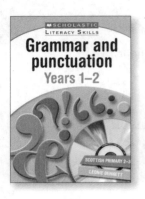

ISBN 978-1407-10045-6

ISBN 978-1407-10046-3

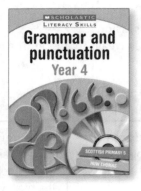

ISBN 978-1407-10047-0

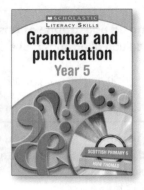

ISBN 978-1407-10048-7

ISBN 978-1407-10049-4

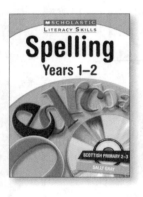

ISBN 978-1407-10055-5

ISBN 978-1407-10056-2

ISBN 978-1407-10057-9

ISBN 978-1407-10058-6

ISBN 978-1407-10059-3

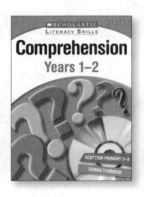

ISBN 978-1407-10050-0

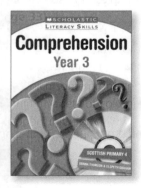

ISBN 978-1407-10051-7

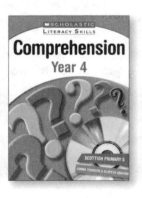

ISBN 978-1407-10052-4

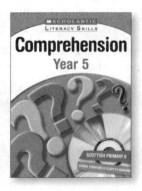

ISBN 978-1407-10053-1

ISBN 978-1407-10054-8

To find out more, call: 0845 603 9091
or visit our website www.scholastic.co.uk